EXTRAORDINARY
TASTE

EXTRAORDINARY TASTE

A Festive Guide For Life After Weight Loss Surgery

Shannon Owens-Malett, MS, RD, LD

LIBRARY OF CONGRESS CONTROL NUMBER: 2008908506

ISBN: HARDCOVER   978-1-4363-7248-0

                 SOFTCOVER   978-1-4363-7247-3

To order additional copies of this book, contact:
Xlibris Corporation
1-888-795-4274
www.Xlibris.com
Orders@Xlibris.com
47621

CONTENTS

Foreword...9

Introduction..11

Nutrition and Weight Loss Surgery 13

Tasty Sips 31

Breakfast Bites..43

Cocktail Bites 65

Poultry and Fish Bites 93

Beef and Pork Bites 133

Salad and Salsa Bites 171

Sweet Bites..199

References..227

Dedication

I thank God for my abilities and gifts.

My accomplishments would not be possible without my devoted husband, amazing daughter and loving family and friends, I am accompanied by your help and encouragement daily.

Let them give thanks to the LORD for his unfailing love and his wonderful deeds for men, for he satisfies the thirsty and fills the hungry with good things.

Psalm 107:8-9 (New International Version)

Foreword

Obesity is a disease, not a personality disorder, with both genetic and environmental causes leading to the accumulation of excess fat, which can be detrimental to health. Weight loss surgery is best thought of as a major push in the right direction in order to achieve reduced weight and subsequent improved health. It is often the push that is needed to overcome years of physiological and psychological barriers that prevent people from losing and keeping off excess weight. However, weight loss surgery is not a magical cure for morbid obesity that requires no effort on the part of the patient in order to achieve weight reduction and subsequent improved health. In fact, the benefits of the surgery can be overcome if dietary and exercise regimens are not adhered to.

Shannon Owens-Malett has been the dietitian in my clinic for the past 5 years and has been indispensable in the care for our patients. In writing this book, Shannon uses her expertise in bariatric nutrition to assist patients in meeting their nutritional needs. She provides dietary guidelines that are garnered from scientific evidence to improve surgical outcome and achieve significant weight reduction while preserving lean muscle tissue. A cookbook written by a dietitian with many years experience in bariatric nutrition is a valuable resource for patients. With this book, patients will have guidance with diet progression, appropriate meal planning, and healthy cooking. Along with vitamin and mineral supplementation, patients using this book will be able to accomplish adequate nutrition during significant weight reduction and weight maintenance. Shannon has done a remarkable job in provided such a great asset for bariatric surgery patients.

David Syn, MD
President of Advanced Bariatric Surgery Center

Introduction

Obesity is an epidemic in America with millions who are overweight (BMI >25) or obese (BMI >30). A person is considered morbidly obese once their BMI increases to 40 or their weight reaches over 100 pounds of their ideal body weight. The statistics for morbid obesity continue to rise and the state of obesity worsens. Obesity can lead to several health risks including heart disease, diabetes mellitus, hypertension, stroke, cancer, and premature death. Numerous patients who are morbidly obese are extremely challenged to lose weight with diet and exercise alone. Many undergo bariatric or Weight Loss Surgery (WLS) as a treatment option. As research continues bariatric surgery could be a treatment option for metabolic diseases and conditions as well. These include diabetes mellitus, hypertension, high cholesterol and more.

Bariatric surgery reduces the size of the stomach, with or without a change in the intestinal absorption of food to achieve rapid weight loss. There are 2 types of bariatric surgery practiced today: purely restrictive and combined restrictive/malabsorptive. The restrictive procedures limit the amount of food a person can eat. The combined restrictive/malabsorptive surgeries limit food consumption and the amounts of food absorbed. The bariatric surgery patient must understand a lifestyle change is essential for weight loss and long-term success.

After WLS, it is necessary to change dietary habits to ensure proper nutrition. The stomach will hold smaller portions and some areas where nutrients are absorbed may be bypassed following the procedure. The WLS diet MUST contain high-quality nutrients. Because of these changes, bariatric surgery patients have Extraordinary Taste . . . a specialized diet and can only consume small amounts to eat and drink.

Life changes considerably after WLS. This is an absolute positive change, where patients are able to enjoy their life! Part of life is festivities, holidays, celebrations, and social events where eating may occur. Many patients have anxiety regarding their new responsibilities to eat properly while attending/hosting parties, holidays, potlucks, etc. This cookbook offers solution and should calm these anxieties. It includes recipes for everyday cooking for bariatric surgery patients and their families. They are simple, elegant, and nutritious. For entertaining events, the recipes can be multiplied easily, and include a festive tip to add enjoyment and finesse. WLS patients should feel confident and take pleasure in attending/hosting parties, celebrations, and other festivities.

This cookbook also includes dietary guidelines, recommended food lists, sample menus, and patient testimonials to aid in understanding the WLS diet. The recipes can be blended for the first stages after surgery. Some modifications to the recipes may be necessary until spices, acidic, and gassy foods are well tolerated. Use this cookbook as a guide for healthy eating with a festive element included for life after WLS.

*It is recommended to follow your surgeon's/dietitian's guidelines that could differ slightly from the guidelines stated in this book.

Nutrition and Weight Loss Surgery

The weight loss surgery should be used as a tool for weight reduction. Take hold of this opportunity and achieve a healthy lifestyle. Behavior changes will be essential for losing and maintaining weight. Following a meal plan, taking supplements, and exercise play an important role for success after surgery.

Weight Loss Surgery Dietary Guidelines

The months following surgery will be a time to learn to eat again and a time for healing. There may be food sensitivities and intolerances that require modification of the diet. Many dietary changes will be discussed in order to develop long-term health and well being.

- 6 small meals daily—eat every 2-3 hours to consume adequate nutrition and feel satisfied with small portions.

- Clear liquid diet (1-2 days after surgery)—broths, sugar-free gelatins, and clear liquid protein supplements.

- Full liquid diet (2 days-2 weeks after surgery)—dairy & soy milk products and protein supplements.

- Blended diet (2 weeks-1 month after surgery)—place foods in a blender with liquids (broth, water, milk) and blend before eating.

- Soft diet (1 month-2 months after surgery)—include foods that require minimal chewing.

- Solid diet (2 months after surgery)—begin adding more variety to protein sources as tolerated.

- Stop drinking liquids 30 minutes before, during, and 30 minutes after meals—drinking at your meal time can make you feel full too soon or can flush foods through your stomach too quickly.

- Consume 64 oz of fluid a day—helps prevent and/or alleviate constipation and is needed for hydration.

- Take small sips of fluid in between meals. Avoid gulping.

- Take small bites and chew thoroughly to applesauce consistency.

- Stop eating or drinking when feelings of fullness occur.

- Use caution with spicy, acidic, and/or gassy foods until tolerance is established.

- Avoid fatty/greasy foods.

- Avoid concentrated sweets and refined carbohydrates (foods made with white flour)—they may cause the DUMPING SYNDROME (nausea, vomiting, cramping, diarrhea, rapid heart beat, weakness, etc.).

- Avoid foods with more than 2 gm sugar alcohol—sorbitol, mannitol, malitol, xylitol, etc. These may also cause dumping syndrome.

- Protein—the emphasis of the diet due to risk of malnutrition. Eat a protein source at every meal and consume it first.

  - Protein supplement (protein powders or ready to drink products)—use these supplements to help consume adequate protein in the beginning months after surgery
  - Best types are whey or soy protein isolates and egg protein powders
  - Find a supplement that is 10 gm carbohydrate or less, 3 gm sugar or less, 2 gm fat or less, and 15 gm protein or more.

- Starch—use high fiber starches. It may take some time to incorporate starches because of intolerance. As the meal portion increases, starches may be added to a protein source.

- Dairy products—use lower fat products. Counts as a protein and carbohydrate source.

- Fruits—it may take some time to incorporate fruits because of intolerance. As the meal portion increases, fruits may be added to a protein source.

- Vegetables—it may take some time to incorporate vegetables because of intolerance. As the meal portion increases, vegetables may be added to a protein source.

- Fat—use only small amounts as they are high calorie. Foods, such as, nuts, nut butters, canola & olive oils, and avocadoes are healthy sources of fat. Avoid fried foods, whole milk dairy products, and fatty meats. Choose lower fat products when able.

- Vitamins/Minerals

    - Multivitamin (adult chewable or liquid)
    - Calcium citrate with vitamin D
    - B-Complex

- Exercise—work up to 20 minutes of walking 2x/day and no lifting more than 10 lbs. in the first 8 weeks after surgery. Discuss exercise regimens with your surgeon.

Tips for Dining Out

- Eating out should not occur until you are confident with food tolerances.
- Plan ahead and know what food to order before dining out. Use a calorie counting book to help determine appropriate foods.
- Ask for a to-go box when you order and put away ⅔-¾ of portion before eating.
- Order from child's or senior citizen's menu.
- Avoid regular salad dressings, sour creams, cream sauces, and gravies.
- Choose foods that are grilled, baked, broiled, or steamed.

Hello. My name is Kristy Owens. I had the Roux-en-Y Gastric Bypass Surgery in December of 2006. I lost 135 lbs and went from a size 24W to a size 4, all in about 18 months.

I've always been simpler in my cooking and eating habits . . . whatever I could just heat up and eat, was good for me!! While there have been a few changes (types of food, checking the ingredients and nutritional analysis, etc.) my cooking habits haven't had to change that much. There are still plenty of "easy" things to prepare!! Turkey chili with some fat-free shredded cheese, lunch meats rolled around some cheese, apples with peanut butter, etc.

When people from work would decide to have a "Food Day", I found I was still able to participate. I would usually make a dessert like banana pudding or some kind of chocolate pudding dish using sugar-free pudding and sugar-free whipped topping and throwing in some unflavored protein powder. I would wait to add the Nilla wafers until I had scooped out my portion. On the chocolate pudding, I would sprinkle chocolate protein powder for that little extra "flavor".

List of Foods for Full Liquid Diet

2 days-2 weeks after surgery

Food Group	Foods Recommended	Foods to Avoid
Protein	Low-fat cottage cheese, low-fat, no added sugar yogurt, sugar-free pudding, skim or 1% milk, light, no added sugar soy milk products, and protein supplements	Whole milk dairy products and dairy products with added sugar, regular soy milk products or soy milk products with added sugar
Carbohydrate	Low-fat, no added sugar dairy products	Cereals and potatoes
Soups	Broth and low-fat cream soups	Regular cream soups or soups made with high fat meats and/or starch
Sweets	Artificial sweeteners	Foods sweetened with regular sugar, foods with more than 2 gm sugar alcohol
Beverages	Sugar-free, non-carbonated beverages, sugar-free popsicles, sugar-free gelatin, and small amount of coffee or tea	Alcohol, carbonated beverages, fruit juice, sugar sweetened drinks, and large amounts of caffeine

*These are suggestions for diet progression. Please follow the advice of your surgeon and dietitian.

Sample Menu for Full Liquid Diet

2 days-2 weeks after surgery

Monday	Tuesday	Wednesday	Thursday	Friday	Saturday	Sunday
Breakfast	*Breakfast*	*Breakfast*	*Breakfast*	*Breakfast*	*Breakfast*	*Breakfast*
¼c low-fat cottage cheese	¼c low-fat, no added sugar yogurt	¼c skim milk mixed with protein supplement	¼c sugar-free pudding mixed with protein supplement	¼c nonfat plain yogurt mixed with vanilla flavored protein supplement	¼c skim milk mixed with protein supplement	¼c low-fat cottage cheese mixed with sugar-free gelatin mix
Snack	*Snack*	*Snack*	*Snack*	*Snack*	*Snack*	*Snack*
¼c skim milk mixed with protein supplement	¼c sugar-free pudding mixed with protein supplement	¼c low-fat cream soup mixed with natural flavored protein supplement	¼c skim milk mixed with protein supplement	¼c low-fat, no added sugar yogurt	¼c sugar-free pudding mixed with protein supplement	¼c skim milk mixed with protein supplement
Lunch	*Lunch*	*Lunch*	*Lunch*	*Lunch*	*Lunch*	*Lunch*
¼c low-fat cream soup mixed with natural flavored protein supplement	¼c low-fat cottage cheese	¼c skim milk mixed with protein supplement	¼c low-fat cottage cheese mixed with sugar-free gelatin mix	¼c sugar-free pudding mixed with protein supplement	¼c low-fat cream soup mixed with natural flavored protein supplement	¼c low-fat, no added sugar yogurt
Snack	*Snack*	*Snack*	*Snack*	*Snack*	*Snack*	*Snack*
¼c sugar-free pudding mixed with protein supplement	¼c low-fat cream soup mixed with natural flavored protein supplement	¼c low-fat cottage cheese	¼c broth mixed with natural flavored protein supplement	¼c low-fat cream soup mixed with natural flavored protein supplement	¼c skim milk mixed with protein supplement	¼c nonfat plain yogurt mixed with vanilla flavored protein supplement

Dinner	*Dinner*	*Dinner*	*Dinner*	*Dinner*	*Dinner*	*Dinner*
¼ c	¼ c	¼ c	¼ c	¼ c	¼ c	¼ c
low-fat, no added sugar yogurt	broth mixed with natural flavored protein supplement	nonfat plain yogurt mixed with vanilla flavored protein supplement	skim milk mixed with protein supplement	broth mixed with natural flavored protein supplement	low-fat cottage cheese	low-fat cream soup mixed with natural flavored protein supplement
Snack	*Snack*	*Snack*	*Snack*	*Snack*	*Snack*	*Snack*
¼ c	¼ c	¼ c	¼ c	¼ c	¼ c	¼ c
nonfat plain yogurt mixed with vanilla flavored protein supplement	skim milk mixed with protein supplement	sugar-free pudding mixed with protein supplement	broth mixed with natural flavored protein supplement	sugar-free pudding mixed with protein supplement	broth mixed with natural flavored protein supplement	skim milk mixed with protein supplement

*These are suggestions for diet progression. Please follow the advice of your surgeon and dietitian.

List of Foods for Blended Diet
2 weeks-1 month after surgery

Food Group	Foods Recommended	Foods to Avoid
Protein	Blended skinless poultry, fish, scrambled eggs, low-fat cottage cheese, low-fat, no added sugar yogurt, sugar-free pudding, skim or 1% milk, light, no added sugar soy milk products, natural peanut butter and protein supplements	Fried, breaded, high-fat meats, skins of meat, tough meats, hard-boiled eggs, nuts, whole milk dairy products and dairy products with added sugar, regular, soy milk products and soy milk products with added sugar
Carbohydrate	Low-fat, no added sugar dairy products	Starches (bread, pasta, rice, cereals, crackers, and potatoes)
Vegetables	Very small amounts of cooked and blended vegetables	Any vegetable that may cause gas or acidic vegetables
Fats	Small amount of canola/olive oil, avocado, olives, low-fat salad dressings, low-fat sour cream, low-fat mayonnaise, light cream cheese, light margarine	Lard, shortening, butter, regular mayonnaise, sour cream, salad dressings, cream cheese, butter
Soups	Broth and low-fat cream soups	Regular cream soups or soups made with high fat meats and/or starch
Sweets	Artificial sweeteners	Foods sweetened with regular sugar, foods with more than 2 gm sugar alcohol
Beverages	Sugar-free, non-carbonated beverages, sugar-free popsicles, sugar-free gelatin, and small amount of coffee or tea	Alcohol, carbonated beverages, fruit juice, sugar sweetened drinks, and large amounts of caffeine

*These are suggestions for diet progression. Please follow the advice of your surgeon and dietitian.

Sample Menu for Blended Diet

2 weeks-1 month after surgery

Monday	Tuesday	Wednesday	Thursday	Friday	Saturday	Sunday
Breakfast	*Breakfast*	*Breakfast*	*Breakfast*	*Breakfast*	*Breakfast*	*Breakfast*
¼c low-fat cottage cheese	¼c low-fat, no added sugar yogurt	1 scrambled egg	¼c nonfat plain yogurt mixed with vanilla flavored protein supplement	1 scrambled egg	¼c-½c skim milk mixed with protein supplement	1 Tbsp natural peanut butter
Snack	*Snack*	*Snack*	*Snack*	*Snack*	*Snack*	*Snack*
¼c-½c skim milk mixed with protein supplement	¼c sugar-free pudding mixed with protein supplement	¼c low-fat cottage cheese mixed with sugar-free gelatin mix	¼c low-fat cottage cheese	¼c-½c low-fat cream soup mixed with natural flavored protein supplement	1 Tbsp natural peanut butter	¼c-½c skim milk mixed with protein supplement
Lunch	*Lunch*	*Lunch*	*Lunch*	*Lunch*	*Lunch*	*Lunch*
¼c blended chicken w/ low-fat cream soup	¼c canned tuna in water w/ low-fat mayonnaise	¼c blended turkey w/ broth	¼c-½c broth mixed with natural flavored protein supplement	¼c low-fat, no added sugar yogurt	¼c blended chicken w/ low-fat cream soup	¼c canned tuna in water w/ low-fat mayonnaise
Snack	*Snack*	*Snack*	*Snack*	*Snack*	*Snack*	*Snack*
¼c low-fat cream soup mixed with natural flavored protein supplement	1 Tbsp natural peanut butter	¼c sugar-free pudding mixed with protein supplement	¼c blended chicken w/ low-fat mayonnaise	¼c blended chicken w/ broth	¼c low-fat cottage cheese	¼c low-fat, no added sugar yogurt

Dinner	Dinner	Dinner	Dinner	Dinner	Dinner	Dinner
¼c canned tuna in water w/ low-fat mayonnaise	¼c blended turkey w/ broth	¼c blended chicken w/ low-fat mayonnaise	¼c blended turkey w/ low-fat cream soup	¼c canned tuna in water w/ low-fat mayonnaise	¼c blended chicken w/ broth	¼c blended turkey w/ low-fat cream soup
Snack	**Snack**	**Snack**	**Snack**	**Snack**	**Snack**	**Snack**
¼c low-fat, no added sugar yogurt	¼c nonfat plain yogurt mixed with vanilla flavored protein supplement	¼c-½c broth mixed with natural flavored protein supplement	1 Tbsp natural peanut butter	¼c-½c skim milk mixed with protein supplement	¼c low-fat, no added sugar yogurt	¼c sugar-free pudding mixed with protein supplement

*These are suggestions for diet progression. Please follow the advice of your surgeon and dietitian.

List of Foods for Soft Diet
1-2 months after surgery

Food Group	Foods Recommended	Foods to Avoid
Protein	Skinless poultry, fish, pork loin, extra lean ground beef, eggs, low-fat cottage cheese, reduced-fat cheese, low-fat, no added sugar yogurt, sugar-free pudding, skim or 1% milk, light, no added sugar soy milk products, natural peanut butter, and protein supplements	Fried, breaded, high-fat meats, skins of meat, tough meats, hard-boiled eggs, nuts, whole milk dairy products and dairy products with added sugar, regular, soy milk products and soy milk products with added sugar
Carbohydrate	Low-fat, no added sugar dairy products	Starches (bread, pasta, rice, cereals, crackers, and potatoes)
Vegetables	Small amounts of cooked vegetables	Regular canned vegetables
Fats	Small amount of canola/olive oil, avocado, olives, low-fat salad dressings, low-fat sour cream, low-fat mayonnaise, light cream cheese, light margarine	Lard, shortening, butter, regular mayonnaise, sour cream, salad dressings, cream cheese, butter
Soups	Broth and low-fat cream soups	Regular cream soups or soups made with high fat meats and/or starch
Sweets	Artificial sweeteners	Foods sweetened with regular sugar, foods with more than 2 gm sugar alcohol
Beverages	Sugar-free, non-carbonated beverages, sugar-free popsicles, sugar-free gelatin, and small amount of coffee or tea	Alcohol, carbonated beverages, fruit juice, sugar sweetened drinks, and large amounts of caffeine

*These are suggestions for diet progression. Please follow the advice of your surgeon and dietitian.

Sample Menu for Soft Diet
1-2 months after surgery

Monday	Tuesday	Wednesday	Thursday	Friday	Saturday	Sunday
Breakfast	**Breakfast**	**Breakfast**	**Breakfast**	**Breakfast**	**Breakfast**	**Breakfast**
¼-½c low-fat cottage cheese	¼-½c low-fat, no added sugar yogurt	¼-½c skim milk mixed with protein supplement	1 soft scrambled egg with ½ oz lean ham	¼-½c sugar-free pudding mixed with protein supplement	1 scrambled egg	1 Tbsp natural peanut butter
Snack	**Snack**	**Snack**	**Snack**	**Snack**	**Snack**	**Snack**
¼-½c broth mixed with natural flavored protein supplement	¼-½c sugar-free pudding mixed with protein supplement	1 Tbsp natural peanut butter	¼-½c low-fat cottage cheese mixed with sugar-free gelatin mix	1 oz reduced-fat cheese	1 Tbsp natural peanut butter	¼-½c low-fat cream soup mixed with natural flavored protein supplement
Lunch	**Lunch**	**Lunch**	**Lunch**	**Lunch**	**Lunch**	**Lunch**
2 oz chicken	¼-½c tuna salad	1 oz turkey 1 oz Swiss cheese	¼-½c skim milk mixed with protein supplement	¼-½c low-fat, no added sugar yogurt	¼-½c chicken salad	¼-½c low-fat cottage cheese
Snack	**Snack**	**Snack**	**Snack**	**Snack**	**Snack**	**Snack**
¼-½c skim milk mixed with protein supplement	2 tsp natural peanut butter mixed with ¼c low-fat, no added sugar vanilla yogurt	¼-½c sugar-free pudding mixed with protein supplement	¼-½c tuna salad	2 oz turkey	¼-½c nonfat plain yogurt mixed with vanilla flavored protein supplement	¼-½c low-fat, no added sugar yogurt

Dinner	*Dinner*	*Dinner*	*Dinner*	*Dinner*	*Dinner*	*Dinner*
2 oz pork loin	2 oz chicken	2 oz fish	2 oz turkey	1 oz chicken	2 oz fish	2 oz pork loin
				1 slice reduced-fat cheese		
Snack	*Snack*	*Snack*	*Snack*	*Snack*	*Snack*	*Snack*
¼-½c low-fat, no added sugar yogurt	¼-½c low-fat cream soup mixed with natural flavored protein supplement	¼-½c nonfat plain yogurt mixed with vanilla flavored protein supplement	1 Tbsp natural peanut butter	¼-½c broth mixed with natural flavored protein supplement	¼-½c sugar-free pudding mixed with protein supplement	¼-½c skim milk mixed with protein supplement

*These are suggestions for diet progression. Please follow the advice of your surgeon and dietitian.

List of Foods for Solid Diet
2 months and more after surgery

Food Group	Foods Recommended	Foods to Avoid
Protein	Skinless poultry, fish, pork loin, extra lean ground beef, beef sirloin, beef jerky, eggs, low-fat cottage cheese, reduced-fat cheese, low-fat, no added sugar yogurt, sugar-free pudding, skim or 1% milk, light, no added sugar soy milk products, natural peanut butter, nuts, and protein supplements	Fried, breaded, high-fat meats, skins of meat, tough meats, whole milk dairy products and dairy products with added sugar, regular, soy milk products and soy milk products with added sugar
Carbohydrate/Starch	Low-fat, no added sugar dairy products, small amount of fruit, whole wheat tortilla, whole wheat bread, brown rice, whole wheat pasta, oats, and other high fiber starches	All refined starches (made with white flour) or carbohydrates with added sugar and/or high fat
Fruits	Fresh, unsweetened frozen or canned fruits in juice or water	Fruits canned in syrup, fruit juices, dried fruits
Vegetables	Fresh, frozen or low-sodium canned vegetables	Regular canned vegetables
Fats	Small amount of canola/olive oil, avocado, olives, low-fat salad dressings, low-fat sour cream, low-fat mayonnaise, light cream cheese, light margarine	Lard, shortening, butter, regular mayonnaise, sour cream, salad dressings, cream cheese, butter
Soups	Broth and low-fat cream soups	Regular cream soups or soups made with high fat meats and/or refined starch

Sweets	Artificial sweeteners	Foods sweetened with regular sugar, foods with more than 2 gm sugar alcohol
Beverages	Sugar-free, non-carbonated beverages, sugar-free popsicles, sugar-free gelatin, and small amount of coffee or tea	Alcohol, carbonated beverages, fruit juice, sugar sweetened drinks, and large amounts of caffeine

*These are suggestions for diet progression. Please follow the advice of your surgeon and dietitian.

Sample Menu for Solid Diet
2 months and more after surgery
EAT PROTEIN FIRST AT EVERY MEAL

Monday	Tuesday	Wednesday	Thursday	Friday	Saturday	Sunday
Breakfast	**Breakfast**	**Breakfast**	**Breakfast**	**Breakfast**	**Breakfast**	**Breakfast**
1 egg omelet w/ 1-2 oz reduced fat cheese	½c-1c low-fat, no added sugar yogurt	½c-1c skim milk	¼c-½c oatmeal made w/ ½c-1c skim milk	½c-¾c low-fat cottage cheese ¼c peaches	1 soft scrambled egg w/ 1 oz diced lean ham	1-2 Tbsp natural peanut butter ¼c unsweetened applesauce
Snack	**Snack**	**Snack**	**Snack**	**Snack**	**Snack**	**Snack**
½c-1c skim milk	½c-1c sugar-free pudding	¼c-¾c low-fat, no added sugar yogurt ¼c strawberries	¼c-¾c low-fat cottage cheese ¼c pears	½c-1c sugar-free pudding	½-1 oz almonds	2-3oz turkey 1oz Swiss cheese
Lunch	**Lunch**	**Lunch**	**Lunch**	**Lunch**	**Lunch**	**Lunch**
2-3 oz chicken ¼-½c salad vegetables w/ low-fat dressing	¼c-¾c tuna salad 3-5 carrot/celery sticks	2-3 oz turkey 1 oz Swiss cheese 1 lettuce leaf	1-2 Tbsp natural peanut butter 2-3 whole wheat crackers	¼c-½c fat-free refried beans ½ whole wheat tortilla	¼c-¾c chicken salad ¼c blueberries	¼c-¾c low-fat cottage cheese ¼c peaches
Snack	**Snack**	**Snack**	**Snack**	**Snack**	**Snack**	**Snack**
½-1 oz nuts	½c-1c low fat, no added sugar yogurt	½c-1c sugar-free pudding	¼c-¾c tuna salad ¼c sliced cucumbers	2-3 oz chicken ¼c strawberries	¼c-¾c low-fat cottage cheese ¼c diced tomatoes	¼c-¾c low-fat, no added sugar yogurt ½c salad vegetables w/low-fat dressing

Dinner	*Dinner*	*Dinner*	*Dinner*	*Dinner*	*Dinner*	*Dinner*
2-3 oz pork loin	2-3 oz extra lean ground beef	2-3 oz fish	2-3 oz chicken	2-3 oz turkey	1 hard boiled egg	½c low fat chili
¼c green beans	¼c mixed vegetables	¼c brown rice	¼c salsa	1 slice reduced-fat cheese	¼c-½c salad vegetables w/low-fat dressing	2-3 whole wheat crackers
Snack	*Snack*	*Snack*	*Snack*	*Snack*	*Snack*	*Snack*
½c-1c low-fat, no added sugar yogurt	½-1 oz nuts	¼-¾c low-fat cottage cheese	½c-1c sugar-free pudding	½c-1c skim milk	1-2 oz reduced-fat cheese	2-3 oz turkey
		¼c pears			½ whole wheat tortilla	½c unsweetened applesauce

*These are suggestions for diet progression. Please follow the advice of your surgeon and dietitian.

The reason I choose to have the weight loss surgery (WLS) was mainly due to my fatty liver. After failing all the diet programs, I researched WLS online. I knew that WLS was my only hope. I had the surgery on September 20, 2006.

At 5'2", I started this process weighing in at 283 lbs, fitting into a 48 size pants, and 3X in shirts. Sad to say, but the only exercise I got was walking fast to get into the buffet line.

Today, I weigh in at 161 lbs (down 122 lbs), wear a size 32 pants, and a small in men's shirts. My fitness program consists of attending BodyPump classes 3 days a week, and walking two miles on the treadmill 3-4 days a week.

My energy and self-confidence levels after WLS continue to grow. I'm completing my MBA and plan to complete the PhD program in addition to working a full and part-time job. My wife and three kids are so proud of me.

My diet consists of six small meals packed high with protein, doctor recommended daily vitamins, and lots of tea and water. Foods and drinks with high sugar contents are not part of my diet. In fact, I have not had a slice of pie or piece of cake or a candy bar since WLS. During office parties, family cookouts, and gatherings (Thanksgiving and Christmas), I pass on the sweets and eat mostly high protein foods such as turkey, chicken or steaks.

Tasty Sips

Ginger Vanilla Lemonade
Mojito Sipper
Watermelon Cooler
Almond Tea
Lemon Lime Punch
Halloween Punch
Spiced Tea Mix
Creamy Hot Cocoa Mix
Cranberry Orange Drink
Eggnog

4 years ago I was a very unhealthy, morbidly obese person. Today I am healthy and active and feel better than I did 20 years ago.

There is so much misinformation about gastric bypass surgery. Some people believe that you can no longer eat your favorite foods, or you have to quit socializing all together. People often ask me if it was difficult to 'give up food'. I don't feel like I gave up anything, but the bondage of the excess weight. Having gastric bypass surgery doesn't mean that you have to give up food. It simply means that you give up 'dieting'. You now have a tool to help you follow a healthy food plan. Foods that are high in fats and sugars are no longer pleasurable, and healthy foods actually taste better.

After having the surgery you will find that you have to be very honest with yourself and your relationship with food. This relationship will change. The challenge will be in being creative and not feeling deprived. When going to events that center around food I take something that is on my meal plan, and I am always pleased with how others enjoy it. With this surgery I have gained a tool that puts me in control of my food choices.

Ginger Vanilla Lemonade

Festive tip:

Serve over full glass of ice. Thread a lemon wedge, mint leaf, and slice of ginger onto a toothpick and set on top of ice in each glass.

3" piece fresh ginger, peeled and sliced
5 cups water
1 cup lemon juice
1 cup Splenda®
2 tsp vanilla extract

In a blender, puree ginger and water. Pour into a pitcher. Add lemon juice, Splenda®, and vanilla extract. Stir well and refrigerate for 1 hour. Strain through cheesecloth before serving.

Yield: ~12 servings

Serving size: ½ cup lemonade

Nutrient Analysis per serving: 16 calories, 0 gm protein, 0 gm carbohydrate, 0 gm fat, 0 gm fiber.

Mojito Sipper

Serve drink in a clear glass and use a tall colorful straw to accent this drink.

¼ cup lime juice
2 Tbsp Splenda®
4-6 mint leaves, divided
Ice
1½ cups water, divided
Lime wedges

In a small bowl, combine lime juice and Splenda®; stir until well mixed. In another small bowl, firmly mash 4 mint leaves, ~30-45 seconds. Add mint to lime juice mixture.

Divide lime juice mixture between 2-8oz glasses. Add ice to each glass until half full. Add ~¾ cup water to each glass and top with ice, if needed. Garnish with remaining mint leaves and lime wedges.

Yield: 2 servings

Serving size: 8 oz sipper

Nutrient analysis per serving: 15 calories, 0 gm protein, 4 gm carbohydrate, 0 gm fat, .25 gm fiber

Watermelon Cooler

Festive tip:

Garnish glass with small watermelon cube and lime zest curl.

4 cups seeded, cubed watermelon
6 cups water
⅓ cup Splenda®
⅓ cup lime juice
Ice

In a food processor, puree watermelon. In a pitcher, combine pureed watermelon with the remaining ingredients and mix well.

Yield: 18 servings

Serving size: ~ ½ cup cooler

Nutrient analysis per serving: 13 calories, .25 gm protein, 3 gm carbohydrate, 0 gm fat, .25 gm fiber

Almond Tea

Festive tip:

Garnish pitcher with lemon slices and mint leaves. Also try tea warm by using 6 cups boiling water and ¼ cup Splenda® instead of amounts in recipe and eliminate ice.

2 family size tea bags
5 cups boiling water
⅓ cup Splenda®
1 Tbsp almond extract
1 Tbsp lemon juice
2 tsp vanilla extract
3 cups ice
2 lemons, sliced

In a large saucepan, brew tea bags in hot water for 3-4 minutes. Remove tea bags. Add Splenda®, almond extract, lemon juice, and vanilla extract and stir well.

In a small pitcher, add ice and lemon slices, squeezing juice from them. Pour tea into pitcher and serve.

Yield: ~16 servings

Serving size: ½ cup tea

Nutrient analysis per serving: 8 calories, 0 gm protein, 1 gm carbohydrate, 0 gm fat, 0 gm fiber

Lemon Lime Punch

Festive tip:

Cut 3 large limes and 3 large lemons into wedges. Remove peel.

Pour 1 cup distilled water into large ring mold lightly coated with non-stick cooking spray. Place peels, peel side up, in ring mold. Freeze until frozen through. Gradually add enough water to fill mold; freeze until frozen through, ~3 hours

Dip bottom of mold in pan of warm water until loosened. Serve punch in punch bowl and float ice ring, fruit side up, in cold punch.

8 cups water
¾ cup lemon juice
¼ cup lime juice
1¼ cups Splenda®
Ice
Lemon and lime wedges

In a pitcher, combine the 1st 4 ingredients and stir. Chill thoroughly. Serve in 8 oz glasses filled with ice and top with lemon and lime wedges.

Yield: ~9 servings

Serving size: 8 oz punch

Nutrient analysis per serving: 18 calories, 0 gm protein, 5 gm carbohydrate, 0 gm fat, 0 gm fiber

Halloween Punch

Festive tip:

Place dry ice in bottom of punch bowl to create a Witches Brew effect.

48 frozen strawberries
Water
1 (.3 oz) package sugar-free orange gelatin mix
2 cups boiling water
8 cups prepared sugar-free wild strawberry drink
Ice

Place strawberries in 3 ice cube trays. Fill with water and freeze until frozen through, ~3 hours.

In a large punch bowl, dissolve gelatin mix in boiling water and stir until gelatin dissolves. Add strawberry drink and ice. Add ice periodically to keep punch cool. Serve punch in glasses with strawberry ice cubes.

Yield: 20 servings

Serving size: ½ cup punch with 2 strawberry ice cubes

Nutrient analysis per serving: 10 calories, .25 gm protein, 2 gm carbohydrate, 0 gm fat, .25 gm fiber

Spiced Tea Mix

Festive tip:

Serve in a clear tea cup with a cinnamon stick. Garnish rim of tea cup with a lemon zest curl.

2 (16 gm) tubs sugar-free lemon drink mix
2 (16 gm) tubs sugar-free orange drink mix
¼ cup Splenda®
3 Tbsp unsweetened instant tea
¾ tsp cinnamon
½ tsp ground cloves
½ tsp allspice

In a medium bowl, combine all ingredients and store tightly covered. Use 1 tsp of tea mix with 8 oz boiling water.

Yield: ~34 servings

Serving size: 1 tsp mix

Nutrient analysis per serving: 7 calories, 0 gm protein, .25 gm carbohydrate, 0 gm fat, 0 gm fiber

Creamy Hot Cocoa

Festive tip:

Add 2 Tbsp coffee granules and only 3 Tbsp cocoa to make a Hot Mocha Mix.

¾ cup Splenda®
½ cup powdered non-dairy creamer
½ cup instant nonfat dry milk
⅓ cup unsweetened cocoa
1½ tsp cinnamon

In a large bowl, combine all ingredients and store tightly covered. Use 2-3 Tbsp cocoa mix with 8 oz boiling water.

Yield: ~16 servings

Serving size: 2 Tbsp cocoa mix

Nutrient analysis per serving: 32 calories, 1 gm protein, 5 gm carbohydrate, 1 gm fat, .75 gm fiber

Cranberry Orange Drink

Festive tip:

Serve in clear glass goblet. Place orange slices in glass. Garnish rim of glass with a small cluster of cranberries.

½ (16 gm) tub or 2 tsp sugar-free cranberry drink mix
½ (16 gm) tub or 2 tsp sugar-free orange drink mix
8 cups water
2 Tbsp lemon juice
1 Tbsp lime juice
3 cinnamon sticks

In a large saucepan, combine all ingredients and bring to a boil. Reduce heat and simmer for 5 minutes. Serve warm or transfer to a container and chill.

Yield: 16 servings

Serving size: ½ cup drink

Nutrient analysis per serving: 6 calories, 0 gm protein, .25 gm carbohydrate, 0 gm fat, 0 gm fiber

Eggnog

Festive tip:

Serve eggnog in punch bowl and sprinkle with nutmeg. Arrange pine cones and Christmas tree ornaments around the bowl.

¼ cup Splenda®
4 cups skim milk, divided
1 (12 oz) can evaporated skim milk
1½ cups fat-free half and half
1 (1 oz) package sugar-free instant vanilla pudding mix
1 tsp vanilla extract
¼ tsp nutmeg

In a large bowl, combine Splenda®, 1½ cups milk, evaporated skim milk, half and half, pudding mix, vanilla extract, and nutmeg. Stir until blended. Chill for several hours. Before serving, add 2½ cups milk and stir well.

Yield: 12 servings

Serving size: ½ cup eggnog

Nutrient Analysis per serving: 83 calories, 5 gm protein, 13 gm carbohydrate, 0 gm fat, 0 gm fiber

Breakfast Bites

High Protein Oatmeal Pancakes
High Protein Waffle
Berries and Cream Crepes
Turkey Sausage
Apple Cinnamon Muesli
Berry Breakfast Smoothie
Sunny Breakfast Fruit Bowl
Breakfast Parfait
Fruity Breakfast Treat
Breakfast Sundae
Sunrise Slushie
Cheesy Breakfast Casserole
Baked Eggs with Light Cream Sauce
Almond Quiche
Ham Scramble
Vegetable Ham Omelet
Spicy Omelet Roll
Cinco de Mayo Breakfast Bake
Avocado Eggs Benedict
Asparagus Frittata

Hi! Chuck and Samantha Andrews here. We have each had Roux-en-Y gastric bypass surgery and have lost a combined 265 lbs. Our surgeries were November 2006 and December 2005. Chuck has gone from a 50 to a 32 inch waist and I have gone from a size 24W to a size 4.

I enjoy cooking and do everything possible to make our new eating lifestyle even more enjoyable than our previous one. My family still eats a wide variety of foods and rarely, if ever, feel as if we are "sacrificing" taste, selection or variety. I highly recommend using fresh herbs and spices, either grown yourself or purchased at the store. Fresh makes a tremendous difference!

My office frequently brings food for celebrations and, of course, there are countless family gatherings, reunions and holidays. I always tuck a protein bar into my purse so we're sure to have a healthy choice but it's usually not necessary. We can almost always find fresh fruit and veggies, slice of lean turkey or ham, maybe a cube or two of cheese or even shrimp or seafood on some buffets. We just leave the sauces and dips behind and enjoy the food itself.

High Protein Oatmeal Pancakes

Festive tip:

Serve pancakes with sugar-free raspberry preserves and fresh kiwi, quartered OR serve with no added sugar cherry pie filling and sugar-free whipped topping.

½ cup quick cooking oats
½ cup whole wheat flour
¼ cup natural flavored protein powder
1 Tbsp Splenda®
½ tsp baking soda
½ tsp cinnamon
1 egg
1 cup buttermilk
2 Tbsp + 1 tsp canola oil, divided

In a medium bowl, combine oats, flour, protein powder, Splenda®, baking soda, and cinnamon and mix well. In a small bowl, combine egg, buttermilk, and 2 Tbsp canola oil and mix well. Stir egg mixture into oats mixture just until moistened.

Pour ⅓ cup batter onto hot skillet or griddle brushed with 1 tsp oil. Turn pancake when batter begins to bubble; cook until golden brown. Repeat with remaining batter.

Top with fresh fruit, Splenda®, or sugar-free preserves.

Yield: 5 servings

Serving size: 1 pancake

Nutrient analysis per serving: 188 calories, 7 gm protein, 17 gm carbohydrate, 11 gm fat, 2 gm fiber

*Great source of fiber and healthy fat

High Protein Waffle

Festive tip:

Use fun-shaped cookie cutters to make waffles different shapes. Top waffles with fresh berries and a dollop of sugar-free whipped topping.

1 cup whole wheat flour
½ cup natural flavored protein powder
2 Tbsp Splenda®
2 tsp baking powder
1 tsp baking soda
½ tsp salt
¼ tsp ground nutmeg
1 egg, separated
1¼ cups water
1 Tbsp canola oil
¼ tsp vanilla extract
Sugar-free preserves

In a large bowl, combine the 1st 7 ingredients. Preheat waffle iron to medium heat. In a small bowl, beat egg white until stiff peaks form. In a medium bowl, beat egg yolk, water, oil, and vanilla extract. Stir egg yolk mixture into flour mixture. Fold in egg white. Pour ½ of mixture onto waffle iron and bake 2-3 minutes or until golden brown. Repeat with remaining batter. Serve with sugar-free preserves.

Yield: 8 servings

Serving size: ¼th waffle

Nutrient analysis per serving: 123 calories, 10 gm protein, 15 gm carbohydrate, 3 gm fat, 2 gm fiber

*Great source of fiber

Berries and Cream Crepes

Festive tip:

Serve on a colorful plate with a dollop of cream filling on the side topped with mint sprig.

⅓ cup whole wheat flour
1 Tbsp Splenda®
⅛ tsp salt
⅛ tsp cinnamon
⅛ tsp orange zest
1 egg
¼ cup skim milk
¼ cup water
4 tsp canola oil, divided
2 Tbsp fat-free sour cream
2 Tbsp fat-free cream cheese, softened
4 tsp sugar-free strawberry preserves, divided
1-2 fresh strawberries, sliced

In a small bowl, combine flour, Splenda®, salt, cinnamon, and orange zest and mix well. In another bowl, mix egg, milk, water, and 2 tsp canola oil. Add egg mixture slowly to flour mixture stirring constantly.

In a small skillet, heat 1 tsp oil to med-high heat. Pour ½ of batter in skillet and tilt pan so batter coats the surface. Cook ~2-3 minutes or until lightly browned. Turn using spatula and cook other side ~2-3 minutes. Repeat using remaining batter. Remove to plate and keep warm.

In a small bowl, blend sour cream and cream cheese. Carefully spread ½ cheese mixture, then 2 tsp preserves, and top with 2 Tbsp strawberry slices onto each crepe. Roll up and serve.

Yield: ~4 servings

Serving size: ½ crepe

Nutrient analysis per serving: 116 calories, 4.5 gm protein, 12 gm carbohydrate, 5.5 gm fat, 1.5 gm fiber

*Good source of fiber and healthy fat

Turkey Sausage

1 Tbsp rubbed sage
2 tsp Splenda®
1¼ tsp salt
½ tsp allspice
¼-½ tsp cayenne pepper
1 lb extra lean ground turkey
¼ tsp maple extract
1 tsp canola oil

In a medium bowl, combine sage, Splenda®, salt, allspice, and cayenne pepper and mix well. Add turkey and maple extract; mix well. Shape into 8 small patties. In a medium skillet lightly brushed with oil, cook over medium heat ~7-8 minutes on each side or until meat is no longer pink.

Yield: 8 servings

Serving size: 1 (2 oz) patty

Nutrient analysis per serving: 203 calories, 16 gm protein, .5 gm carbohydrate, 10 gm fat, 0 gm fiber

Apple Cinnamon Muesli

Festive tip:

In parfait glasses, alternate layers of muesli, fruit, nuts, and yogurt.

1 cup rolled oats
1 cup water
1 cup shredded apple with skin
¼ cup Splenda®
2 Tbsp natural flavored protein powder
2 Tbsp lemon juice
½ tsp cinnamon
Fresh fruit
Chopped pecans
Dollop nonfat plain yogurt

In a large bowl, combine oats, water, apple, Splenda®, protein powder, lemon juice, and cinnamon and mix well. Cover and refrigerate overnight.

To serve, spoon ¼-½ cup muesli into bowl and top with fruit, pecans, and yogurt, if desired.

Yield: ~4 servings

Serving size: ½ cup muesli, 1 tsp pecans, and 1 Tbsp yogurt

Nutrient analysis per serving: 138 calories, 8 gm protein, 21 gm carbohydrate, 4 gm fat, 3 gm fiber.

*Excellent source of fiber and healthy fat

Berry Breakfast Smoothie

Festive tip:

Thread 4-5 fresh blueberries on a small wooden skewer and place over the rim of the glass.

1 cup skim milk
½ cup frozen mixed berries, thawed
2 Tbsp natural flavored protein powder
2 Tbsp Splenda®
⅛ tsp orange extract
2 ice cubes

In a blender, combine the 1st 5 ingredients and pulse until smooth. Add ice and pulse until thick and smooth. Pour into serving glass.

Yield: 4 servings

Serving size: ½ cup smoothie

Nutrient analysis per serving: 62 calories, 8 gm protein, 6 gm carbohydrate, .5 gm fat, 1 gm fiber

*Good source of fiber

Sunny Breakfast Fruit Bowl

2 cups cantaloupe
2 med apples, cored and cut into 1" pieces
10 large strawberries, sliced
1 cup seedless grapes
2 small kiwis, peeled and sliced
1½ cups nonfat plain yogurt
2 Tbsp lemon juice
2 Tbsp natural flavored protein powder
½ tsp sugar-free breakfast orange drink mix

In a large bowl, combine fruit. In a small bowl, mix yogurt, lemon juice, protein powder, and drink mix until smooth. Drizzle yogurt mixture over fruit and toss gently.

Yield: 12 servings

Serving size: ½ cup fruit bowl

Nutrient analysis per serving: 61 calories, 3 gm protein, 12 gm carbohydrate, .25 gm fat, 2 gm fiber

*Great source of fiber

Breakfast Parfait

Festive tip:

Serve parfait with a dollop of sugar-free whipped topping. Sprinkle with sunflower seeds and garnish rim of glass with a kiwi slice.

2 cups nonfat plain yogurt
⅓ cup Splenda®
2 kiwis, peeled and sliced
½ cup sunflower seed kernels
1 cup fresh berries
2 Tbsp sugar-free whipped topping

In a medium bowl, combine yogurt and Splenda® and mix well. In 2 parfait glasses, divide 1 cup yogurt mixture for bottom layers. Add layers of kiwi slices, sunflower seeds, remaining yogurt mixture, and berries for each parfait. Top each with 1 Tbsp whipped topping.

Yield: 6 servings

Serving size: ⅓ parfait

Nutrient analysis per serving: 115 calories, 6 gm protein, 19 gm carbohydrate, 1.25 gm fat, 2 gm fiber

*Great source of fiber and healthy fat

Fruity Breakfast Treat

Festive tip:

Serve breakfast treat in a short stemmed wine glass. Set glass on a doily-lined plate. Garnish glass with a kiwi slice and red straw.

2 strawberries, chopped
1 small apple, peeled, cored, and chopped
1 small mango, peeled, seeded, and chopped
1 kiwi, peeled and chopped
⅓ cup prepared sugar-free lemonade
½ cup light soy milk
1 cup sugar-free whipped topping
1 Tbsp natural flavored protein powder

In a blender, combine the 1st 4 ingredients and pulse until smooth. Add lemonade and pulse 2-3 times. Add milk, whipped topping, and protein powder and pulse until smooth.

Yield: 8 servings

Serving size: ½ cup treat

Nutrient analysis per serving: 55 calories, 2 gm protein, 10 gm carbohydrate, 1 gm fat, 1 gm fiber

*Good source of fiber

Breakfast Sundae

1 Tbsp natural peanut butter
2 strawberries, sliced
1 (4 oz) container low carbohydrate vanilla yogurt
1 Tbsp sugar-free strawberry preserves, melted in microwave
1 Tbsp chopped pecans

In a small glass bowl, spread peanut butter to cover the bottom. Place strawberry slices over peanut butter, and spoon yogurt on top of strawberries. Drizzle with strawberry preserves and top with pecans.

*This recipe used Dannon® Light and Fit sugar/carb control yogurt.

Yield: 1 serving

Serving size: 1 sundae

Nutrient analysis per serving: 225 calories, 10 gm protein, 15 gm carbohydrate, 16 gm fat, 2.5 gm fiber

*Great source of fiber and healthy fat

Sunrise Slushie

Festive tip:

Serve in margarita glasses with bright pink straws. Garnish rim of glass with orange slices and a cherry with stem.

½ cup water
½ cup prepared sugar-free orangeade (This recipe used Minute Maid® Light)
¼ cup sugar-free apricot preserves
1 (4 oz) container low carbohydrate vanilla yogurt
1 Tbsp Splenda®
1 Tbsp natural flavored protein powder
¼ tsp banana extract
10-12 ice cubes

In a blender, combine water, orangeade, apricot preserves, yogurt, Splenda®, protein powder, and banana extract. Pulse until smooth. Gradually add ice and pulse until mixture is smooth. Pour into chilled glasses.

*This recipe used Dannon® Light and Fit sugar/carb control yogurt.

Yield: ~6 servings

Serving size: ½ cup slushie

Nutrient analysis per serving: 24 calories, 2 gm protein, 4 gm carbohydrate, .5 gm fat, 0 gm fiber

Cheesy Breakfast Casserole

1 dozen eggs
½ cup evaporated skim milk
1 tsp salt
1 tsp pepper
1 tsp ground mustard
½ cup low-fat cottage cheese
1 cup cubed fully cooked lean ham
1 small tomato, diced
¾ cup reduced-fat shredded cheddar cheese

In a large bowl, whisk together eggs, evaporated skim milk, salt, pepper, mustard, and cottage cheese. Stir in ham and tomato. Sprinkle cheese onto bottom of a 9 x 13 baking dish coated with nonstick cooking spray. Pour egg mixture over cheese.

Bake @ 325° for 65-75 minutes or until firm. Let cool 5 minutes. Cut into squares before serving.

Yield: 12 servings

Serving size: 1/12th casserole

Nutrient analysis per serving: 108 calories, 10 gm protein, 2 gm carbohydrate, 6 gm fat, 0 gm fiber

Festive tip:

Take lean ham slices and fill 4 muffin tins with a ham slice. Break eggs into ham cups instead of custard cups.

Baked Egg with Light Cream Sauce

4 eggs
¼ cup light cream
¼ tsp salt
¼ tsp minced chives
¼ tsp pepper
Diced tomato
Parsley sprigs

Break eggs into 4 custard cups coated with nonstick cooking spray. In a small bowl, beat cream, salt, chives, and pepper until well mixed. Spoon 1 Tbsp cream sauce over each egg. Place custard cups on a cookie sheet.

Bake @ 350° for 20-25 minutes or until whites have set and become opaque. Garnish with tomato and parsley sprigs.

Yield: 4 servings

Serving size: 1 baked egg

Nutrient analysis per serving: 103 calories, 7 gm protein, 1 gm carbohydrate, 7 gm fat, 0 gm fiber

Almond Quiche

Festive tip:

Serve with fresh raspberries and garnish with watercress.

2 Tbsp chopped onion
1 garlic clove, minced
2 tsp olive oil
2 eggs
1½ cups skim milk
2 Tbsp whole wheat flour
1 Tbsp fresh parsley, minced
½ tsp salt
½ tsp ground mustard
¼ tsp white pepper
½ cup shredded Swiss cheese
½ cup shredded Parmesan cheese
½ cup sliced almonds

In a small skillet, sauté onions and garlic in oil for 1-2 minutes or until tender. In a large bowl, beat eggs, milk, flour, parsley, salt, mustard, and pepper until light and fluffy. Stir in sautéed onion and garlic and cheeses.

Line a 9" pie plate with almonds and pour egg mixture over almonds. Cover and bake @ 375° for 40 minutes or until knife inserted in middle comes out clean. Uncover and let brown slightly, ~10 minutes. Let stand for 10 minutes. Slice and serve.

Yield: 8 servings

Serving size: ⅛th quiche

Nutrient analysis per serving: 120 calories, 6 gm protein, 5 gm carbohydrate, 7 gm fat, 1 gm fiber

*Good source of fiber and healthy fat

Ham Scramble

Festive tip:

Serve casserole over salad greens and garnish with whole ripe olives and grape tomatoes.

1 Tbsp chopped onion
1 Tbsp chopped mushroom
1 Tbsp canola oil
1 cup cubed fully cooked lean ham
½ cup frozen spinach, thawed and squeezed dry
4 eggs
1 Tbsp skim milk
¼ tsp salt
¼ tsp pepper
½ cup reduced-fat shredded cheddar cheese

In a large skillet, sauté onion and mushroom in oil until tender. Stir ham and spinach into skillet and remove from heat. In a medium bowl, whisk eggs, milk, salt, and pepper together. Pour egg mixture into skillet and return to medium heat. Cook stirring constantly until eggs are set. Top with cheese. Serve immediately.

Yield: ~4 servings

Serving size: ¼th ham scramble

Nutrient analysis per serving: 141 calories, 9 gm protein, 3 gm carbohydrate, 10 gm fat, 1 gm fiber

*Good source of fiber and healthy fat

Vegetable Ham Omelet

1 Tbsp chopped zucchini
1 Tbsp chopped onion
3 tsp canola oil, divided
½ cup egg whites or egg substitute
1 Tbsp skim milk
¼ tsp salt
¼ tsp pepper
⅓ cup diced fully cooked lean ham
1 Tbsp diced tomato
2 Tbsp reduced-fat shredded cheddar cheese

In a small skillet, sauté zucchini and onion in 1 tsp oil until tender crisp. Set aside and keep warm. In a small bowl, mix together egg whites, milk, salt, and pepper. In a medium skillet, bring remaining oil to med-high heat. Cook egg mixture; as the eggs set, lift the edges to allow uncooked mixture to run underneath and cook. Add ham, tomato, sautéed vegetables, and cheese on top of egg. When eggs are cooked completely, gently fold edge over. Move to plate and let stand for ~2 minutes.

Yield: 2 servings

Serving size: ½ omelet

Nutrient analysis per serving: 191 calories, 19 gm protein, 3.5 gm carbohydrate, 11 gm fat, .25 gm fiber

*Good source of healthy fat

Spicy Omelet Roll

Festive tip:

Serve on a bright colored plate with a side of pico de gallo. Sprinkle with fresh cilantro.

4 eggs
¼ tsp basil
¼ tsp pepper
⅛ tsp salt
¼ cup reduced-fat shredded cheddar cheese
¼ cup diced fully cooked lean ham
1 Tbsp chopped onion
1 Tbsp diced jalapeno pepper
2 tsp skim milk
1 Tbsp olive oil

In a medium bowl, beat eggs, basil, pepper, and salt until well mixed. In a small bowl, combine cheese, ham, onion, jalapeno, and milk and mix well. In a large skillet, bring oil to med-high heat and cook egg mixture. As eggs set, lift edges to allow uncooked mixture to run underneath and cook. Place cheese mixture in the middle of the egg. When eggs are cooked completely, gently fold eggs over top and bottom of cheese and press and hold for a few seconds. Fold sides over and press and hold for a few seconds. Cut into slices and serve.

Yield: 4 servings

Serving size: ¼th omelet roll

Nutrient analysis per serving: 124 calories, 9 gm protein, 1 gm carbohydrate, 10 gm fat, 0 gm fiber

*Good source of healthy fat

Cinco de Mayo Breakfast Bake

Festive tip:

Serve breakfast bake
on white plate with
black bean salsa
and avocado slices.
Garnish plate with
a serrano pepper
and tomatillo. To
be extra festive,
sprinkle confetti and
streamers on serving
table.

2 (4 oz) cans chopped green chiles, drained and divided
1 cup reduced-fat shredded sharp cheddar cheese
1 cup reduced-fat shredded mild cheddar cheese
6 eggs
½ cup evaporated skim milk
1 tsp salt
½ tsp cumin
½ tsp basil
½ tsp pepper

Place 1 can of chiles in the bottom of a 9 x 13 baking dish coated with nonstick cooking spray. Top with 1 cup cheese. Place the other can of chiles onto cheese layer and top with remaining cheese. In a medium bowl, beat eggs with evaporated skim milk until light. Add salt, cumin, basil, and pepper and beat until well mixed. Pour over cheese layer. Bake @ 350° for 30-35 minutes or until firm.

Yield: 12 servings

Serving size: 1/12th egg bake

Nutrient analysis per serving: 95 calories, 9 gm protein, 2.5 gm carbohydrate, 5.5 gm fat, .5 gm fiber

Avocado Eggs Benedict

Festive tip:

Variations of Eggs
Benedict: Use sliced
turkey breast, turkey
sausage or smoked
salmon instead of
ham. Add a grilled
tomato slice, diced
jalapeno peppers
and/or sliced onion.
Serve over ½ slice
whole wheat toast
or ½ whole wheat
tortilla.

2 whole wheat English muffins, split and toasted
4 slices of fully cooked lean ham
4 eggs, poached
4 thin avocado slices, ~½ an avocado

Sauce

¼ cup fat-free sour cream
¼ cup fat-free mayonnaise
1 tsp prepared mustard
1 tsp lemon juice
¼ tsp salt
¼ tsp pepper
Dash paprika
Parsley sprigs

Place ½ English muffin on 4 hot plates. Top each English muffin with ham, then egg, and finally avocado slice. In a small sauce pan, combine sour cream, mayonnaise, mustard, lemon juice, salt, and pepper. Mix well and heat through. Spoon sauce over avocado slice and sprinkle with paprika. Garnish with parsley sprigs.

Yield: 4 servings

Serving size: 1 egg Benedict with 1-2 Tbsp sauce

Nutrient analysis per serving: 233 calories, 14 gm protein, 22 gm carbohydrate, 11 gm fat, 4 gm fiber

*Excellent source of fiber and healthy fat

Asparagus Frittata

5 large eggs
½ cup skim milk
¼ cup + 2 Tbsp reduced-fat shredded sharp cheddar cheese, divided
1 tsp ground mustard
½ tsp salt
½ tsp pepper
1 Tbsp olive oil
2 Tbsp chopped onion
¼ lb asparagus, trimmed and cut diagonally into 1" pieces

Preheat oven to broil. In a large bowl, whisk eggs, milk, ¼ cup cheese, mustard, salt, and pepper until well mixed. In an oven-proof skillet, bring oil to med-high heat. Add onion and asparagus, cook, stirring frequently, until crisp tender, ~3 minutes.

Reduce to low heat and pour egg mixture into skillet. Cook stirring a few times, until eggs are well set around the edges, but still loose in the center. Sprinkle with remaining cheese. Place skillet 4-6" under broiler in oven and cook until frittata is puffed, browned, and cooked through, ~3-4 minutes. Let stand 5 minutes.

Yield: ~5 servings

Serving size: 1/5th frittata

Nutrient analysis per serving: 132 calories, 10 gm protein, 3 gm carbohydrate, 9 gm fat, .5 gm fiber

*Good source of healthy fat

Cocktail Bites

Fiesta Pepper Bites
Crab and Artichoke Stuffed Mushrooms
Salmon and Cream Cheese Stuffed Tomatoes
Pizza Pie
Pizza Dip
Creamy Spinach Dip
Black Bean Dip
Layered Dip
Chickpea Dip (Hummus)
Hot Artichoke Dip
Vegetable Dip
Satay Dip
Pumpkin Seeds
Sweetened Almonds
Grape and Nut Mix
Asian Spiced Nut Mix
Pimento Cheese Spread
Bacon Cheese Spread
Chicken Cheese Ball
Seafood Ball
Stuffed Banana Peppers
Chicken Stuffed Celery
Parsley Tuna Snacks
Deviled Eggs
Hot Pepper Jelly

I thank God Jehovah and my Savior Jesus Christ for leading me by His Holy Spirit to my surgeon and weight loss surgery. My life and health has never been better or the same since my bariatric surgery in June 2006. I am now able to enjoy a full quality life with my spouse and children. I can now travel pain free to visit my family and friends. Due to remission of sarcoidosis, I no longer experience swelling nor shortness of breath. My blood pressure has stabilized and blood sugars are regulated by diet.

I am truly grateful for the nutrition class because my eating habits are much better. I now eat for health rather than for the reasons I ate before. I simply can't think of enough words to thank my God for all my surgeon and his staff did to assist me on this 2 year journey back to excellent health.

If weight is your problem, I highly recommend you have weight loss surgery. I am a satisfied client with a weight loss of 110 lbs in 14 months.

Fiesta Pepper Bites

Festive tip:

Serve on a white plate with a side of salsa. Garnish with fresh cilantro.

1 medium orange pepper
1 medium green pepper
1 medium red pepper
1½ tsp canola oil, divided
1 garlic clove, minced
½ cup chopped onion
1 lb extra lean ground beef
½ tsp salt
½ tsp pepper
1 cup reduced-fat shredded cheddar cheese
1 small tomato, diced

Slice each pepper into quarters and scrape seeds out. Cut each quarter in half. In a large skillet, sauté pepper "chips" in 1 tsp oil over med-high heat for ~2 minutes. Place pepper "chips" in a 9 x 13 baking dish coated with nonstick cooking spray.

In the same skillet, cook garlic and onion in remaining oil. Add ground beef, salt, and pepper and cook ~5 minutes or until no longer pink. Spoon beef mixture onto each pepper chip. Top with cheese. Bake @ 400° for ~8 minutes until cheese is melted. Top with tomato.

Yield: 12 servings

Serving size: 2 pepper bites

Nutrient analysis per serving: 134 calories, 12 gm protein, 2 gm carbohydrate, 8 gm fat, .5 gm fiber

Crab and Artichoke Stuffed Mushrooms

20-24 med mushrooms
1 Tbsp olive oil
Salt and pepper, to taste
1 (6 oz) can artichoke hearts, in water or brine, drained and chopped
1 (4 oz) can imitation crab meat, drained
½ cup shredded Parmesan cheese
2 Tbsp low-fat mayonnaise
1 celery stalk, diced
1 Tbsp finely chopped onion
1 tsp parsley
¼ tsp garlic salt
¼ tsp coarse ground pepper

Remove stems from mushrooms. In a large skillet, heat oil to med-high heat and cook mushroom caps ~2-3 minutes on each side. Set mushrooms on a plate round side down. Sprinkle with salt and pepper. In a medium bowl, mix remaining ingredients and spoon into mushroom caps.

Yield: 12 servings

Serving size: 2 mushrooms

Nutrient Analysis per serving: 66 calories, 6 gm protein, 4 gm carbohydrate, 3 gm fat, .25 gm fiber

Salmon and Cream Cheese Stuffed Tomatoes

18 cherry tomatoes
3 oz canned, boneless salmon, drained
2 oz light cream cheese
1 Tbsp finely chopped celery
⅛ tsp salt
⅛ tsp dill
Dash pepper
Paprika

Cut the tops off tomatoes. Scrap seeds and pulp out. Drain tomatoes well on a paper towel. In a small bowl, combine salmon, cream cheese, celery, salt, dill, and pepper and mix well. Spoon mixture into tomatoes. Sprinkle with paprika.

Yield: 9 servings

Serving size: 2 tomatoes

Nutrient analysis per serving: 40 calories, 3 gm protein, 2 gm carbohydrate, 2 gm fat, .5 gm fiber

Pizza Pie

Festive tip:

Serve pizza pie on a white plate. Fill condiment bottle with tomato sauce and make wavy lines with tomato sauce on outer rim of plate. Sprinkle fresh oregano leaves on top of tomato sauce.

½ cup whole wheat flour
3 Tbsp grated Parmesan cheese, divided
1 Tbsp skim milk
1 tsp olive oil
1 egg, slightly beaten
⅛ tsp garlic powder
⅛ tsp oregano
½ cup tomato sauce
½ cup shredded mozzarella cheese made with part skim milk
8 slices turkey pepperoni

In a medium bowl, combine flour and 1½ Tbsp Parmesan cheese and mix well. In a small bowl, combine milk, oil, and egg and mix well. Add milk mixture to flour mixture and mix until a soft dough forms. Press dough onto bottom and sides of a 1 Qt baking dish coated with nonstick cooking spray. Bake @ 375° for 15 minutes.

Sprinkle with garlic powder, oregano, and remaining Parmesan cheese. Spread tomato sauce on top. Sprinkle with mozzarella cheese and place pepperoni slices on top. Bake for an additional 15 minutes or until cheese is melted. Let stand 10 minutes before cutting.

Yield: 4 servings

Serving size: ¼th pizza pie

Nutrient analysis per serving: 116 calories, 7 gm protein, 13.5 gm carbohydrate, 4 gm fat, 2 gm fiber

*Great source of fiber

Pizza Dip

Festive tip:

Place pie plate on a lettuce-lined serving platter and garnish dip with fresh basil leaves.

1 (8 oz) package light cream cheese
¼ cup low-fat sour cream
2 Tbsp skim milk
¼ tsp Italian seasoning
⅛ tsp garlic powder
½ cup tomato sauce
¼ cup chopped green pepper
1 Tbsp chopped green onion
1 Tbsp sliced ripe olives
½ cup shredded mozzarella cheese made with part skim milk
Melba toast

In a medium bowl, combine the 1st 5 ingredients and spread onto the bottom of a 9" pie plate. Top with tomato sauce, green pepper, green onion, and olives. Sprinkle with cheese. Bake @ 400° for 10-12 minutes. Serve with Melba toast.

Yield: ~8-9 servings

Serving size: ¼ cup dip with 3 Melba toast crackers

Nutrient analysis per serving: 136 calories, 6 gm protein, 15 gm carbohydrate, 6 gm fat, 1.5 gm fiber

*Good source of fiber

Creamy Spinach Dip

1 (8 oz) package light cream cheese
½ cup low-fat sour cream
½ cup frozen spinach, thawed and squeezed dry
1 (4 oz) can sliced water chestnuts, drained and chopped
¼ cup reduced-fat shredded Colby Jack cheese
2 Tbsp shredded beef jerky
1 tsp dill
¼ tsp garlic salt
⅛ tsp pepper
Fresh vegetables

In a large bowl, beat cream cheese and sour cream until smooth. Add spinach, water chestnuts, cheese, beef jerky, dill, garlic salt, and pepper and mix well. Spread dip into a 9" pie plate. Serve with vegetables.

Yield: 10 servings

Serving size: ¼ cup dip with ¼ cup fresh vegetables

Nutrient analysis per serving: 90 calories, 4 gm protein, 5.5 gm carbohydrate, 5 gm fat, 1 gm fiber

*Good source of fiber

Black Bean Dip

Festive tip:

Cut vegetables into 2" strips and place them upright in a small glass or beaker and serve beside dip.

1 small tomato, chopped and seeded
½ cup chopped onion
1 jalapeno pepper, chopped and seeded
1 garlic clove, chopped
1 (15 oz) can black beans, rinsed and drained
2 Tbsp lime juice
1 tsp cilantro
1 tsp cumin
¾ tsp salt
½ tsp pepper
½ cup low-fat sour cream
½ cup reduced-fat shredded Pepper Jack cheese
Fresh vegetables

In a food processor, combine tomato, onion, jalapeno, and garlic and pulse until finely chopped. Add beans, lime juice, cilantro, cumin, salt, and pepper; pulse until smooth. Stir in sour cream and cheese. Spoon into a 1 Qt baking dish. Bake @ 375° for 20 minutes. Serve with fresh vegetables.

Yield: 7 servings

Serving size: ½ cup dip with ¼ cup vegetables

Nutrient analysis per serving: 92 calories, 5 gm protein, 16.5 gm carbohydrate, 1 gm fat, 5 gm fiber

*Excellent source of fiber

Layered Dip

Festive tip:

Place dip dish on a large plate. Surround dip dish with assorted colors of bell pepper slices and baked tortilla chips. Garnish dip with fresh jalapeno slices.

1 lb extra lean ground turkey
½ cup chopped onion
½ tsp garlic salt
¼ tsp chili powder
1 (14 oz) can fat-free refried beans
¾ cup reduced-fat shredded cheddar cheese
¾ cup low-fat sour cream
1 cup shredded lettuce
1 small tomato, diced
2 Tbsp sliced ripe olives
Bell pepper slices
Baked tortilla chips

In a large skillet, combine turkey, onion, garlic salt, and chili powder and cook over med-high heat until meat is no longer pink; drain. In an 8 x 8 dish, spread beans onto bottom. Top with cheese, turkey, sour cream, lettuce, tomato, and olives. Serve with sliced peppers and baked tortilla chips.

Yield: ~28 servings

Serving size: ¼ cup dip with ~4 baked tortilla chips

Nutrient analysis per serving: 91 calories, 7 gm protein, 9.5 gm carbohydrate, 2.75 gm fat, 1.25 gm fiber

*Good source of fiber

Chickpea Dip (Hummus)

Festive tip:

Spoon hummus
in white shallow
bowl. Use the round
side of a spoon
and hollow out the
middle of the dip.
Fill the middle with
whole chickpeas.
On the outer edge
of dip, sprinkle a
section with paprika
then with fresh
chopped parsley.
Continue to alternate
paprika and fresh
chopped parsley
around the entire
outer edge of dip.

1 (15 oz) can chickpeas or Garbanzo beans, rinsed and
drained
3 Tbsp lemon juice
2 Tbsp olive oil
¼ cup water
1 garlic clove, minced
½ tsp salt
½ tsp pepper
⅛ tsp cayenne pepper
Fresh chopped parsley
Fresh vegetables

In a food processor, combine chickpeas, lemon juice, oil, water,
and garlic and pulse until finely chopped. Add salt, pepper, and
cayenne pepper. Pulse until well blended. Garnish with parsley.
Serve with carrots, celery, grape tomatoes, and cucumbers slices.

Yield: 10 servings

Serving size: ¼ cup dip with ¼ cup vegetables

Nutrient analysis per serving: 83 calories, 3.5 gm protein, 9.5
gm carbohydrate, 3.5 gm fat, 3 gm fiber

*Excellent source of fiber and healthy fat

Hot Artichoke Dip

Festive tip:

Place dip in a colorful bowl. Slice a carrot and place slices on top of dip around the edge of the bowl. Sprinkle with chopped green chiles.

1 (13 oz) jar artichoke hearts in brine, drained
2 Tbsp chopped onion
1 garlic clove, minced
1 Tbsp olive oil
1 (4 oz) can chopped green chiles, drained
1 (8 oz) package light cream cheese
½ cup low-fat sour cream
¼ cup shredded Parmesan cheese
½ tsp Creole seasoning
½ cup shredded mozzarella cheese made with part skim milk
Fresh vegetables

In a large skillet, sauté artichoke, onion, and garlic in oil until tender. Add green chiles to skillet and stir. Set aside and keep warm. In a large bowl, beat cream cheese, sour cream, Parmesan cheese, and Creole seasoning. Stir cream cheese mixture into artichoke mixture and return to heat. Heat through. Add mozzarella cheese and heat until bubbly. Serve with assorted vegetables.

Yield: 17 servings

Serving size: ¼ cup dip with ¼ cup vegetables

Nutrient analysis per serving: 88 calories, 5 gm protein, 5.5 gm carbohydrate, 5 gm fat, 1.5 gm fiber

*Good source of fiber

Vegetable Dip

Festive tip:

Serve vegetable dip in small bowl and place on a large plate. Take several cucumber slices, a cherry tomato, 2 spinach leaves, 1 small celery stalk, and several baby carrots. Make a flower design beside the dip bowl using celery stalk as the stem, cucumber slices as the flower petals, tomato as the center of the flower, spinach as the stem leaves, and carrots as the grass around the flower.

½ cup nonfat plain yogurt
¾ cup low-fat sour cream
1 Tbsp chopped green onion
1 Tbsp capers
½ tsp lemon juice
¼ tsp Worcestershire sauce
¼ tsp Dijon mustard
¼ tsp garlic salt
¼ tsp dill
¼ tsp salt
Fresh vegetables

In a medium bowl, combine the 1st 10 ingredients and mix well. Cover and refrigerate for 1 hour. Serve with vegetables.

Yield: 5 servings

Serving size: ¼ cup dip with ¼ cup vegetables

Nutrient analysis per serving: 79 calories, 5 gm protein, 6.5 gm carbohydrate, 3 gm fat, 1 gm fiber

*Good source of fiber

Satay Dip

Festive tip:

Serve dip in a glass and set in the middle of a serving platter. Arrange skewered chicken and vegetables around the dip.

½ cup finely chopped onion
1 garlic clove, minced
1 Tbsp red pepper flakes
2 tsp olive oil
2 tsp sesame oil
¼ cup Splenda®
2 Tbsp lemon juice
2 Tbsp red wine vinegar
2 Tbsp soy sauce
1 tsp tomato sauce
½ tsp ground ginger
½ cup natural peanut butter
Skewered chicken
Fresh vegetables

In a large skillet, sauté onion, garlic, and red pepper flakes in oils until tender. Add Splenda®, lemon juice, vinegar, soy sauce, tomato sauce, and ginger and mix well. Remove from heat and stir in peanut butter. Serve hot with skewered chicken or fresh vegetables.

Yield: 10 servings

Serving size: 2 Tbsp dip with 1 oz chicken

Nutrient analysis per serving: 156 calories, 13 gm protein, 4 gm carbohydrate, 9 gm fat, 1.25 gm fiber

*Good source of fiber and healthy fat

Seasoned Pumpkin Seeds

Festive tip:

Sprinkle pumpkin seeds over low-fat chili, tuna salad or yogurt to add a unique taste.

1½ tsp olive oil
½ tsp garlic salt + garlic salt to taste, if desired
¼ tsp paprika
2 Tbsp lemon juice
1 cup raw pumpkin seeds

In a medium bowl, combine oil, ½ tsp garlic salt, paprika, and lemon juice and mix well. Add pumpkin seeds and toss to coat. Spread seeds in a single layer on a cookie sheet. Sprinkle with a small amount of garlic salt to taste, if desired. Bake @ 300° for 30-35 minutes, stirring occasionally. Let cool. Store in an airtight container.

Yield: 4 servings

Serving size: ¼ cup seeds

Nutrient Analysis per serving: 203 calories, 9 gm protein, 5 gm carbohydrate, 2 gm fat, 2.25 gm fiber

*Great source of fiber and healthy fat

Sweetened Almonds

Festive tip:

On a large platter, make several lines with nuts or make a festive shape with nuts, i.e. Christmas tree, bell, etc.

2 cups salted almonds
¾ cup Splenda®
⅓ cup water
1½ tsp vanilla extract

In a medium saucepan, combine all ingredients. Cook and stir over medium heat until liquid is mostly absorbed, ~15-20 minutes. Place nuts on a cookie sheet coated with nonstick cooking spray. Bake @ 350° for 25 minutes, stirring 3 times. Transfer to a cookie sheet covered with parchment paper and cool. Store in an airtight container.

Yield: 8 servings

Serving size: ¼ cup almonds

Nutrient analysis per serving: 217 calories, 8 gm protein, 9 gm carbohydrate, 18 gm fat, 4 gm fiber

*Excellent source of fiber and healthy fat

Grape and Nut Mix

Festive tip:

Serve nut mix in decorative muffin liners and place on a white serving platter.

½ cup seedless grapes
½ cup All-Bran® cereal
½ cup peanuts
½ cup slivered almonds
½ cup soy nuts
¼ tsp cinnamon

In a large bowl, combine all ingredients and mix well. Serve and refrigerate leftovers.

Yield: 10 servings

Serving size: ¼ cup nut mix

Nutrient analysis per serving: 125 calories, 7 gm protein, 7 gm carbohydrate, 9 gm fat, 5 gm fiber

*Excellent source of fiber and healthy fat

Asian Spiced Nut Mix

1 cup almonds
½ cup pretzels
½ cup sunflower seed kernels
½ cup crisp wheat cereal squares
⅛ tsp garlic powder
¼-½ tsp red ground pepper
2 Tbsp canola oil
2 Tbsp soy sauce

In a large bowl, combine dry ingredients. In a small bowl, combine oil and soy sauce and mix well. Add oil mixture to almond mixture. Toss. Place nut mix on a 15 x 11 baking sheet. Bake @ 250° for 45-50 minutes, stirring occasionally. Let cool. Store in an airtight container.

Yield: 9 servings

Serving size: ½ cup nut mix

Nutrient Analysis per serving: 243 calories, 7.5 gm protein, 16 gm carbohydrate, 18 gm fat, 4 gm fiber

*Excellent source of fiber and healthy fat

Pimento Cheese Spread

Festive tip:

Use other ingredients to make different variations of pimento cheese, such as,

- Fresh chopped jalapeno
- ⅛ tsp ground mustard
- ⅛ tsp wasabi powder
- 1 Tbsp prepared mustard
- 1 Tbsp Worcestershire sauce
- Louisiana hot sauce

4 oz light cream cheese, softened
⅓ cup low-fat mayonnaise
1½ cups reduced-fat shredded sharp cheddar cheese
½ cup reduced-fat shredded Colby Jack cheese
1 (4 oz) jar diced pimentos, drained and mashed
¼ tsp grated onion
½ tsp garlic salt
Cracked pepper to taste
Fresh vegetables

In a large bowl, beat cream cheese and mayonnaise until smooth. Add shredded cheeses, pimentos, onion, garlic salt, and cracked pepper and stir until well blended. Serve with carrots, celery, and other fresh vegetables.

Yield: 10 servings

Serving size: ¼ cup cheese spread with ¼ cup vegetables

Nutrient analysis per serving: 120 calories, 9 gm protein, 5.5 gm carbohydrate, 7 gm fat, 1.25 gm fiber

*Good source of fiber

Bacon Cheese Spread

Festive tip:

Make stuffed chicken breasts. Cut a pocket into the side of the chicken breast. Spoon cheese spread into pocket and close and secure with toothpick. In a large skillet, brown chicken on both sides in a small amount of olive oil. Once browned, place chicken in a baking dish coated with nonstick cooking spray and bake @ 350° ~30-40 minutes or until no longer pink.

1 (8 oz) package light cream cheese, softened
2 tsp white vinegar
½ tsp ground mustard
½ tsp parsley
1 med tomato, seeded and chopped
¼ cup reduced-fat real bacon bits
Fresh vegetables

In a large bowl, beat cream cheese, vinegar, mustard, and parsley until blended. Stir in tomato and bacon bits. Refrigerate for 1 hour. Serve with vegetables.

Yield: 7 servings

Serving size: ¼ cup cheese spread with ¼ cup vegetables

Nutrient analysis per serving: 106 calories, 5.5 gm protein, 5.5 gm carbohydrate, 6.5 gm fat, 1.25 gm fiber

*Good source of fiber

Chicken Cheese Ball

Festive tip:

Serve cheese ball on a black plate. Take 9-10 stuffed olives and thread 1 olive onto the tip of a toothpick. Insert the other side of the toothpick into the base of the cheese ball leaving a small space in between each toothpick.

2 (8 oz) packages light cream cheese, softened
1 (10 oz) can white meat chicken, drained
1 (1 oz) package salad dressing mix
½-¾ cup coarse ground pepper
Fresh vegetables

In a medium bowl, combine the 1st 3 ingredients and mix well. Shape into a ball. On a plate, pour pepper and roll cheese ball in pepper until well-covered. Place cheese ball on a clean serving platter and serve with assorted vegetables.

Yield: 13 servings

Serving size: ¼ cup cheese ball with ¼ cup vegetables

Nutrient analysis per serving: 135 calories, 8 gm protein, 10.5 gm carbohydrate, 7 gm fat, 2.25 gm fiber

*Great source of fiber

Seafood Ball

Festive tip:

Line a white plate with fresh parsley sprigs. Place seafood ball in the middle of plate and pour sauce over seafood ball.

1 (4 oz) can shrimp, drained and pat dry with a paper towel
1 (8 oz) package light cream cheese, softened
½ tsp soy sauce
½ tsp lemon juice
½ tsp seafood seasoning
Lemon wedges
Fresh vegetables

Sauce

½ cup tomato sauce
2 Tbsp Splenda®
2 Tbsp cider vinegar
1 Tbsp prepared horseradish
½ tsp celery seed
½ tsp garlic salt

In a food processor, pulse shrimp until well chopped. In a medium bowl, combine shrimp, cream cheese, soy sauce, lemon juice, and seafood seasoning and mix well. Form into a ball. In a small bowl, combine sauce ingredients and mix well.

Place seafood ball on a clean plate and pour sauce over seafood ball. Garnish with lemon wedges. Serve with assorted vegetables.

Yield: ~8 servings

Serving size: ¼ cup seafood ball, 1½ Tbsp sauce, and ¼ cup vegetables

Nutrient analysis per serving: 102 calories, 7 gm protein, 6 gm carbohydrate, 5 gm fat, 1.5 gm fiber

*Good source of fiber

Stuffed Banana Peppers

Festive tip:

Line black serving platter with carrot and cucumber slices and place stuffed peppers on top of vegetable slices. Put a bowl of low-fat dill sauce in the middle of the plate for dipping.

12 large banana peppers
1 plum tomato, seeded and finely chopped
¼ cup finely chopped onion
¼ cup finely chopped green pepper
2 Tbsp shredded beef jerky
1½ cups reduced-fat shredded cheddar cheese
⅛ tsp salt
⅛ tsp pepper

Slice peppers down the middle and remove seeds. Place pepper halves, rounded side down, on a cookie sheet. In a large bowl, combine remaining ingredients and mix well. Spoon cheese mixture into each pepper half. Bake @ 400° for 30-35 minutes.

Yield: 12 servings

Serving size: 2 stuffed peppers

Nutrient analysis per serving: 57 calories, 5 gm protein, 3 gm carbohydrate, 3 gm fat, 1.5 gm fiber

*Good source of fiber

Chicken Stuffed Celery

1 (5 oz) can white meat chicken, drained
¼ cup crushed pineapple in its own juice, drained
1 tsp parsley
1 tsp minced green onion
½ tsp seasoned salt
4 oz light cream cheese
8 celery stalks, cut into 3" pieces

In a large bowl, combine chicken, pineapple, parsley, green onion, and seasoned salt and mix well. Stir in cream cheese until smooth. Spread chicken mixture onto celery sticks. Cover and chill thoroughly, ~1 hour.

Yield: 12 servings

Serving size: 2 stuffed celery

Nutrient analysis per serving: 41 calories, 3 gm protein, 2 gm carbohydrate, 2 gm fat, .5 gm fiber

Parsley Tuna Snacks

Festive tip:

Serve on a bright
colored plate.
Garnish with tomato
and lemon slices.

2 (7 oz) cans tuna in water, drained and flaked
1 (8 oz) package light cream cheese
1 Tbsp lemon juice
1 tsp prepared horseradish
1 tsp dill
½ tsp salt
½ tsp pepper
1 cup finely chopped fresh parsley

In a large bowl, combine the 1st 7 ingredients and mix well. Shape into small balls, ~18-20. Place parsley on a large plate and roll balls in parsley until lightly coated. Cover and refrigerate ~1 hour.

Yield: 10 servings

Serving size: 2 tuna snacks

Nutrient analysis per serving: 106 calories, 12 gm protein, 2 gm carbohydrate, 5 gm fat, .25 gm fiber

Deviled Eggs

Festive tip:

Make Halloween spider deviled eggs. Place deviled eggs on an orange plate. Take whole black olives, slice them in half. Place one olive half on top of a deviled egg, rounded side up, for the spider body. Take the other olive half and slice into 8 pieces. Place 4 olive slices on each side of the spider body for spider legs.

3 large eggs, hard-boiled
1 Tbsp low-fat mayonnaise
2 tsp low-fat sour cream
1 tsp Splenda®
½ tsp Dijon mustard
½ tsp white vinegar
¼ tsp salt
¼ tsp pepper
¼ tsp dill
Paprika

Slice hard-boiled eggs lengthwise. Remove egg yolks and set egg whites aside. In a small bowl, combine egg yolk, mayonnaise, sour cream, Splenda®, Dijon mustard, vinegar, salt, pepper, and dill and mix well. Pipe or spoon egg yolk mixture into egg whites. Refrigerate. Sprinkle with paprika before serving.

Yield: 6 servings

Serving size: 1 deviled egg

Nutrient analysis per serving: 50 calories, 3 gm protein, .5 gm carbohydrate, 3 gm fat, 0 gm fiber

Hot Pepper Jelly

Festive tip:

Other suggested uses—serve over a burger patty, use small amount in tuna or chicken salad, on top of pork loin, glaze for meats, or make a vinaigrette with 1 Tbsp jelly, 2 Tbsp vinegar, 5 Tbsp olive oil.

4 green peppers, seeded and diced
10 jalapeno peppers, seeded and diced
1 cup vinegar
½ cup lemon juice
4 cups Splenda®
¼ tsp salt
1 (1.75 oz) package No Sugar Needed Fruit Pectin
Green food coloring

In a blender, pulse peppers, vinegar, and lemon juice until pureed. Transfer to a large pot and add Splenda® and salt. Mix well. Bring to a rolling boil; reduce heat and simmer for 10 minutes. Add pectin and food coloring and mix well. Bring to rolling boil for 1 minute. Using hot sterilized half pint jars, ladle pepper mixture to within ¼" from the top. Cover with flat lids and screw bands on tightly.

Place jars into a water bath that completely covers them and bring to a boil. Boil for 15 minutes. Remove from water bath and place in a dark, quiet place to cool. Jelly may take 24 hours up to 2 weeks to set.

Serve jelly over an 8 oz block of light cream cheese. Garnish with whole grain crackers and assorted vegetables.

Yield: 4-5 half pint jars, ~72 servings

Serving size: 2 Tbsp jelly

Nutrient Analysis per serving: 14 calories, .25 gm protein, 3.5 gm carbohydrate, 0 gm fat, .5 gm fiber

Poultry and Fish Bites

Lemon Chicken Soup
Chicken Stew
Chicken Verde Quiche
Spinach Chicken Bake
Boneless Buffalo Wings
Parsley Chicken Strips
Slice O'Peach Chicken
Nutty-Baked Chicken
Lime Coconut Chicken
Parmesan Chicken
Sweet 'n' Sour Chicken
Swiss Mushroom Chicken
Pineapple Chicken
Turkey and Swiss Wrap
Turkey Barley Stew
White Chili
Turkey Sausage and Red Beans
Apricot Turkey Kielbasa
Turkey Patties
Turkey Meatballs with Basil Cream Sauce
Vegetable Turkey Loaf
Cajun Turkey Tenderloin
Thanksgiving Turkey
Pecan-Crusted Shrimp
Apricot-Glazed Shrimp
Shrimp Scampi
Pan-Seared Sea Scallops
Shrimp Lettuce Wraps
Fish Tacos with Garlic Tartar Sauce
Crab Salad Bites
Stuffed Sole with Dill Sauce
Baked Tilapia with Cucumber Sauce
Balsamic-Glazed Salmon
Grilled Citrus Halibut
Tuna Steaks with Garlic Lime Sauce

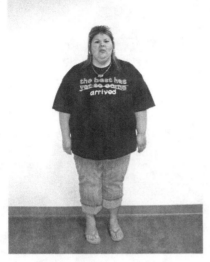

My name is Minerva and I had weight loss surgery, WLS, in September 2006. I have lost 242 lbs in 23 months and went from a size 52 to a size 8. I was always overweight and never thought I would be a small size. I thank my surgeon and WLS for saving my life! People who pass by me don't even recognize me. I have no regrets with having the surgery except I wish I would have had it sooner. I'm starting a whole new life!

After having surgery, I had to read books to learn how to eat healthier foods. I thought "Why did I have the surgery if I am going to go back to eating the same way?" I watch my calories and include exercise, such as, walking 3 days a week and Zumba 2 days a week.

When I am invited to a party, I always ask "What can I bring?" because being Hispanic there can be many fried foods. I usually take some veggies or lean meats so that I can eat something healthy. I also carry my own water bottle or something like Crystal Light and some nuts just in case. I have learned how to make foods healthy, like stuffed jalapeños; I use fat-free cream cheese and turkey bacon. My family and friends are eating healthier because of foods that I take. This is the best decision I ever made!

Lemon Chicken Soup

Festive tip:

Serve soup in white bowls, top with a lemon slice and a pinch of minced fresh parsley.

2 (6 oz) skinless chicken breasts, cut into 1" pieces
¼ tsp salt
1 Tbsp canola oil
1 (15 oz) can chicken broth
1 (10.75 oz) low-fat, reduced-sodium cream of chicken soup, condensed
¼ cup lemon juice
½ cup fresh torn spinach
¼ cup shredded carrots
¼ cup chopped celery
2 Tbsp chopped onion
1 tsp Butterbuds®
Pepper to taste
3 egg yolks

Sprinkle chicken with salt. In a Dutch oven, bring oil to med-high heat and cook chicken until no longer pink. Add broth, soup, lemon juice, vegetables, Butterbuds®, and pepper and stir well.

In a small bowl, lightly whisk yolks. Slowly stir a small amount of broth mixture into egg yolks. Gradually add egg mixture into soup, stirring constantly. Bring to boil. Reduce heat and simmer until vegetables are tender, ~20 minutes.

Yield: ~9 servings

Serving size: ½ cup soup

Nutrient analysis per serving: 123 calories, 14 gm protein, 3 gm carbohydrate, 5 gm fat, .75 gm fiber

Chicken Stew

Festive tip:

In a black bowl, serve stew over small amount of couscous. Place bowl on a colorful plate and garnish plate with green pepper slices. Garnish stew with fresh basil leaves.

2 (6 oz) skinless chicken breasts, cut into 1" pieces
2 tsp canola oil
1 (15 oz) can chicken broth
½ cup chopped onion
½ cup chopped green pepper
½ cup frozen corn, thawed
1 celery rib, chopped
1 (14 oz) can Great Northern beans, rinsed and drained
1 (14 oz) can diced tomatoes, drained
¼ tsp garlic powder
½ tsp salt
½ tsp pepper
¼ tsp basil
1 bay leaf

In a Dutch oven, bring oil to med-high heat and cook chicken ~6-8 minutes or until no longer pink. Add remaining ingredients and bring to boil. Cover and simmer 30 minutes-1 hour. Remove bay leaf before serving.

Yield: 13 servings

Serving size: ½ cup stew

Nutrient analysis per serving: 78 calories, 7 gm protein, 10 gm carbohydrate, 1 gm fat, 2 gm fiber

*Great source of fiber

Chicken Verde Quiche

Festive tip:

Place quiche dish on a colorful plate. Garnish the center of quiche with diced tomatoes and green chiles. Place parsley sprig atop tomatoes and green chiles.

4 eggs
8 whole wheat crackers, crushed
¼ tsp baking powder
¾ cup low-fat cottage cheese
½ cup reduced-fat shredded cheddar cheese
1 (4 oz) can green chiles, drained
1 (6 oz) skinless chicken breast, cooked and cubed

In a large bowl, combine eggs, cracker crumbs, and baking powder until well mixed. Fold in other ingredients. Place in a 1 Qt baking dish coated with nonstick cooking spray. Bake @ 350° for 65-75 minutes or until toothpick inserted in middle comes out clean. Let stand 5 minutes before serving.

Yield: ~5 servings

Serving size: 1/5th quiche

Nutrient analysis per serving: 200 calories, 24 gm protein, 7 gm carbohydrate, 8 gm fat, 1 gm fiber

*Good source of fiber

Festive tip:

Place chicken bake dish on a colorful plate and sprinkle with paprika and fresh spinach leaves.

Spinach Chicken Bake

1 cup cooked skinless chicken breast, cubed
¼ cup reduced-fat shredded cheddar cheese
¼ cup frozen spinach, thawed and squeezed dry
1 Tbsp finely chopped green onion
1 egg
¼ cup skim milk
½ cup low-fat sour cream
¼ tsp seasoned salt
¼ tsp pepper
⅛ tsp cayenne pepper

In a medium bowl, combine the 1st 4 ingredients; mix well and spoon into a 1 Qt baking dish coated with nonstick cooking spray. In a medium bowl, whisk egg, milk, sour cream, salt, pepper, and cayenne pepper and pour over chicken mixture. Bake @ 350° for ~40 minutes or until bubbly and slightly browned.

Yield: 5 servings

Serving size: 1/5th chicken bake

Nutrient analysis per serving: 130 calories, 15 gm protein, 2 gm carbohydrate, 6 gm fat, .5 gm fiber

Boneless Buffalo Wings

1 lb skinless chicken strips
2 Tbsp canola oil
¼ cup Louisiana-style hot sauce
¼ cup tomato sauce
2 Tbsp water
2 Tbsp cider vinegar
1 Tbsp Splenda®
1 tsp butter extract
1 tsp chili powder
½ tsp salt
½ tsp pepper
1 garlic clove, minced
Reduced-fat blue cheese salad dressing
Celery sticks

In a large skillet, cook chicken in oil over med-high heat stirring frequently for 4-6 minutes or until no longer pink. In a small bowl, combine hot sauce, tomato sauce, water, vinegar, Splenda®, butter extract, chili powder, salt, pepper, and garlic and mix well. Add hot sauce mixture to chicken. Cook, covered, over low heat for 15-20 minutes. Serve with salad dressing and celery sticks.

Yield: 8 servings

Serving size: 1 chicken strip with 1 Tbsp reduced-fat salad dressing

Nutrient analysis per serving: 132 calories, 19 gm protein, 2 gm carbohydrate, 7 gm fat, .25 gm fiber

*Good source of healthy fat

Parsley Chicken Strips

Festive tip:

Serve chicken strips on a black plate over roasted onions, bell peppers, and mushrooms. Garnish with lime wedges and parsley sprigs.

12 skinless chicken strips
2 Tbsp olive oil, divided
¼ cup whole wheat flour
1 tsp parsley
¾ tsp salt
½ tsp pepper

Brush chicken strips with 1 Tbsp olive oil. In a shallow bowl, combine flour, parsley, salt, and pepper and mix well. Dip chicken strips into flour mixture. In a large skillet, bring remaining oil to med-high heat. Cook chicken strips ~3-4 minutes on each side or until juices run clear.

Yield: 12 servings

Serving size: 1 chicken strip

Nutrient analysis per serving: 122 calories, 18 gm protein, 2 gm carbohydrate, 4 gm fat, .5 gm fiber

*Good source of healthy fat

Slice O'Peach Chicken

Festive tip:

Serve chicken on a black plate with a side of sliced peaches. Garnish with mint sprigs.

2 (6 oz) skinless chicken breasts
½ tsp salt
½ tsp pepper
1 Tbsp canola oil
1 cup water
¼ cup Splenda®
1 (2 oz) package onion soup mix
½ tsp basil
¼ tsp nutmeg
⅛ tsp orange zest
1 (8 oz) can sliced peaches in its own juice, drained

Sprinkle chicken with salt and pepper. In a large skillet, cook chicken in oil over med-high heat for 5-6 minutes on each side or until browned. Place chicken in a 1½ Qt baking dish coated with nonstick cooking spray. In same skillet, combine water, Splenda®, onion soup mix, basil, nutmeg, and orange zest and bring to boil while stirring. Pour onion soup mixture over chicken. Cover and bake @ 375° for 35-40 minutes or until bubbly. Remove cover and place peaches between chicken. Bake, uncovered, another 10-15 minutes.

Yield: 6 servings

Serving size: 2 oz chicken with 2 Tbsp peaches and sauce

Nutrient analysis per serving: 138 calories, 18 gm protein, 6 gm carbohydrate, 4 gm fat, .25 gm fiber

*Good source of healthy fat

Nutty-Baked Chicken

Festive tip:

Serve on a colorful plate, sprinkle chicken with Parmesan cheese and a dash of Creole seasoning. Garnish plate with almonds and parsley sprigs.

⅔ cup ground almonds
¼ cup grated Parmesan cheese
¾ tsp Creole seasoning
1 Tbsp canola oil
2 (6 oz) skinless chicken breasts

In a shallow bowl, combine the 1st 3 ingredients and mix well. Brush chicken with oil and coat chicken in nut mixture. Place chicken in a 9 x 13 baking dish coated with nonstick cooking spray. Bake @ 350° for 45 minutes or until no longer pink.

Yield: 6 servings

Serving size: 2 oz chicken

Nutrient analysis per serving: 210 calories, 22 gm protein, 3 gm carbohydrate, 13 gm fat, 2 gm fiber

*Great source of fiber and healthy fat

Coconut Lime Chicken

Festive tip:

Slice key limes, fan out, and place on top of chicken breast.

¼ cup lime juice
¼ cup water
2 Tbsp olive oil
1 Tbsp Splenda®
1 tsp coconut extract
1 garlic clove, minced
½ tsp salt
½ tsp pepper
¼ tsp cayenne pepper
2 (6 oz) skinless chicken breasts

In a large resealable bag, combine the 1st 9 ingredients. Add chicken and refrigerate ~4 hours or overnight. Discard marinade. Grill chicken over med-hot coals ~5 minutes on each side or until no longer pink.

Yield: 6 servings

Serving size: 2 oz chicken

Nutrient analysis per serving: 103 calories, 18 gm protein, 1 gm carbohydrate, 3 gm fat, 0 gm fiber

*Good source of healthy fat

Parmesan Chicken

1 egg, slightly beaten
1 Tbsp skim milk
⅓ cup grated Parmesan cheese
2 Tbsp whole wheat flour
½ tsp salt
½ tsp pepper
½ tsp parsley
2 (6 oz) skinless chicken breasts

In a small bowl, combine egg and milk and mix well. In another small bowl, mix Parmesan cheese, flour, salt, pepper, and parsley. Dip chicken into egg mixture, then coat with Parmesan cheese mixture. Place chicken in a 9 x 13 baking dish coated with nonstick cooking spray. Bake @ 375° for 60-75 minutes or until no longer pink.

Yield: 6 servings

Serving size: 2 oz chicken

Nutrient analysis per serving: 134 calories, 21 gm protein, 2 gm carbohydrate, 4 gm fat, .5gm fiber

Sweet 'n' Sour Chicken

Festive tip:

Serve chicken on
a square black
plate and place red
chopsticks beside
stir-fry.

2 (6 oz) skinless chicken breasts, cut into strips
¼ tsp salt
¼ tsp pepper
2 Tbsp canola oil
1 small carrot, julienned
1 small green pepper, cut into strips
¼ cup chopped onion
1 (4 oz) can sliced water chestnuts, drained
½ cup sugar-free orange marmalade
¼ cup lemon juice
¼ cup soy sauce
¼ tsp garlic powder
¼ tsp ground ginger
⅛ tsp red pepper flakes

Sprinkle chicken with salt and pepper. In a large skillet, bring
oil to med-high heat and cook chicken ~6-8 minutes or until
chicken is no longer pink. Add carrot, green pepper, onion, and
water chestnuts. Cook and stir until vegetables are crisp tender.
In a small bowl, combine orange marmalade, lemon juice, soy
sauce, garlic powder, ginger, and red pepper flakes and mix well.
Stir orange marmalade mixture into chicken and vegetables.
Bring to a boil; cover, and simmer for 10 minutes.

Yield: 6 servings

Serving size: 2 oz chicken, ⅓ cup vegetables, and ~2 Tbsp
sauce

Nutrient analysis per serving: 160 calories, 18 gm protein, 14
gm carbohydrate, 7 gm fat, 1 gm fiber

*Good source of fiber and healthy fat

Swiss Mushroom Chicken

Festive tip:

Sauté a handful of small whole mushrooms and grape tomato halves in 1 Tbsp olive oil. Sprinkle with salt, pepper, and parsley and serve over chicken. Garnish with watercress and an orange slice.

2 (6 oz) skinless chicken breasts
½ tsp salt
½ tsp pepper
¼ tsp Creole seasoning
1 Tbsp olive oil
1 cup chicken broth
½ cup chopped onion
1 garlic clove, chopped
1 (4 oz) can sliced mushrooms, drained
1 (10.75 oz) can low-fat, reduced-sodium cream of mushroom soup, condensed
2 slices Swiss cheese

Sprinkle chicken with salt, pepper, and Creole seasoning. In a large skillet, bring oil to med-high heat and cook chicken 3-4 minutes on each side or until browned. Remove from heat and place in a 9 x 13 baking dish coated with nonstick cooking spray. In same skillet, add chicken broth, onion, garlic, and mushrooms. Cook 2-3 minutes. Stir in mushroom soup and heat through. Pour mixture over chicken and top with cheese slices. Bake @ 375° for 20-25 minutes or until bubbly.

Yield: 6 servings

Serving size: 2 oz chicken with ~4 Tbsp soup

Nutrient analysis per serving: 132 calories, 18 gm protein, 8 gm carbohydrate, 4 gm fat, .75 gm fiber

*Good source of healthy fat

Pineapple Chicken

Festive tip:

Serve chicken on a colorful plate over ¼ cup brown rice. Garnish with lime slices and parsley sprigs.

¼ cup soy sauce
1 (8 oz) can crushed pineapple in its own juice, drained
3 Tbsp canola oil, divided
2 Tbsp water
1 tsp ground ginger
½ tsp orange extract
2 (6 oz) skinless chicken breasts
1 garlic clove, minced
⅓ cup chopped onion

In a large resealable bag, combine soy sauce, pineapple, 2 Tbsp canola oil, water, ginger, and orange extract. Add chicken and refrigerate ~4 hours. In a large skillet, bring remaining oil to med-high heat and sauté garlic and onion until tender. Add chicken, set marinade aside, and cook chicken 3-4 minutes on each side or until no longer pink. Remove chicken and keep warm. Add marinade to skillet and bring to boil; boil on low heat for ~10 minutes. Add chicken to marinade sauce; cover and simmer for 15-20 minutes.

Yield: 6 servings

Serving size: 2 oz chicken with 1-2 Tbsp sauce

Nutrient analysis per serving: 140 calories, 18 gm protein, 6 gm carbohydrate, 7 gm fat, .5 gm fiber

*Good source of healthy fat

Turkey and Swiss Wrap

Festive tip:

Cut turkey wraps
into finger size wraps
and place on serving
platter. Top finger
size wraps with
whole olives secured
by toothpicks.
Garnish platter with
alfalfa sprouts and
cherry tomatoes.

1 (7") whole wheat flour tortilla
1 Tbsp light cream cheese
1 Tbsp shredded beef jerky
¼ tsp parsley
¼ tsp cracked pepper
2 slices Swiss cheese
4 slices deli turkey
2 romaine lettuce leaves
2 thin tomato slices

Spread cream cheese on tortilla. Sprinkle beef jerky, parsley, and
pepper over cream cheese. Top with Swiss cheese, turkey, lettuce,
and tomato. Fold tortilla over and roll it up tightly. Secure with
toothpicks. Cut in half and serve. Cover leftovers in plastic and
refrigerate.

Yield: 2 servings

Serving size: ½ wrap

Nutrient analysis per serving: 161 calories, 20 gm protein, 12
gm carbohydrate, 4 gm fat, 5 gm fiber

*Excellent source of fiber

Turkey Barley Stew

Festive tip:

Serve stew in a red bowl lined with a large lettuce leaf. Top with several purple onion rings and garnish with chopped parsley.

1 lb skinless turkey breasts, cut into 1" pieces
½ tsp salt
½ tsp pepper
1 Tbsp canola oil
½ cup chopped onion
½ cup pearl barley
2 carrots, peeled and sliced
1 celery stalk, chopped
1 (15 oz) can chicken broth
1 (14 oz) can diced tomatoes
1 tsp parsley
½ tsp thyme
1 bay leaf

Sprinkle turkey with salt and pepper. In a Dutch oven, bring oil to med-high heat and cook turkey until no longer pink. Add onion and cook until tender. Add barley, stirring often until slightly browned or toasted. Add carrots and celery and coat well with juices. Stir in broth, tomatoes, parsley, thyme, and bay leaf. Bring to boil; cover and simmer for 45 minutes. Remove bay leaf before serving.

Yield: 15 servings

Serving size: ½ cup stew

Nutrient analysis per serving: 66 calories, 6 gm protein, 5 gm carbohydrate, 2 gm fat, .75 gm fiber

White Chili

1 lb extra lean ground turkey
½ cup chopped onion
1 garlic clove, minced
1 (14 oz) can Great Northern beans, rinsed and drained
1 (10.75 oz) can low-fat, reduced-sodium cream of chicken
soup, condensed
1 (10 oz) can diced tomatoes with green chiles
3 cups water
½ tsp parsley
½ tsp coriander
½ tsp ground red pepper
½ tsp cumin
½ tsp salt
Reduced-fat shredded cheese

In a Dutch oven, cook turkey with onion and garlic until
no longer pink. Stir in beans, soup, tomatoes, water, parsley,
coriander, red pepper, cumin, and salt. Bring to boil and simmer
~45 minutes. Serve in a bowl with cheese sprinkled on top.

Yield: 20 servings

Serving size: ½ cup chili with 1 oz of reduced-fat cheese

Nutrient analysis per serving: 136 calories, 12 gm protein, 7 gm
carbohydrate, 7 gm fat, 1.5 gm fiber

*Good source of fiber

Turkey Sausage and Red Beans

Festive tip:

Serve in colorful bowls and garnish with basil leaves and chopped tomato.

1 lb Italian turkey sausage links
½ cup chopped onion
1 garlic clove, minced
1 (14 oz) can red beans, rinsed and drained
1 (14 oz) can diced tomatoes, drained
½ cup chopped green pepper
1 (15 oz) can chicken broth
1 tsp parsley
½ tsp Creole seasoning
8 Tbsp shredded mozzarella cheese made with part skim milk

In a Dutch oven, cook sausage until browned. Cut sausage into ¼" slices. Add onion and garlic and cook 1-2 minutes; drain. Stir in beans, tomatoes, green pepper, broth, parsley, and Creole seasoning. Bring to a boil; cover and simmer ~40 minutes. Top each serving with 1 Tbsp cheese.

Yield: ~8 servings

Serving size: 2 oz sausage, ¼-½ cup beans, and 1 Tbsp cheese

Nutrient analysis per serving: 146 calories, 13 gm protein, 12 gm carbohydrate, 5 gm fat, 4 gm fiber

*Excellent source of fiber

111

Apricot Turkey Kielbasa Sausage

Festive tip:

Serve sausage on a colorful plate with steamed squash and tomato slices. Garnish with rosemary sprig.

1 lb turkey kielbasa sausage, cut into ¼" slices
½ cup sugar-free apricot preserves
2 Tbsp lemon juice
2 tsp soy sauce
1 tsp Dijon mustard
¼ tsp orange zest
¼ tsp white pepper
¼ tsp cilantro
¼ tsp ground ginger
⅛ tsp garlic powder

In a large skillet, cook sausage until browned; drain. In a medium bowl, combine remaining ingredients; mix well and add to skillet. Heat through, 6-7 minutes. Let stand 5-10 minutes.

Yield: 8 servings

Serving size: 2 oz turkey sausage with ~1 Tbsp sauce

Nutrient analysis per serving: 95 calories, 9 gm protein, 7 gm carbohydrate, 5 gm fat, 0 gm fiber

Turkey Patties

Festive tip:

Serve patties
over peppers and
mushrooms sautéed
in a small amount
of oil. Sprinkle with
chopped parsley.

10-12 whole wheat crackers, crushed
½ cup low-fat sour cream
1 Tbsp chopped green onion
1 tsp balsamic vinegar
½ tsp salt
½ tsp pepper
1 lb extra lean ground turkey
1-2 tsp canola oil

In a large bowl, combine the 1st 6 ingredients and mix well. Crumble turkey over cracker mixture and mix well. Shape into 8 patties. In a large skillet brushed with oil, cook patties over med-high heat for 6-7 minutes on each side or until no longer pink.

Yield: 8 servings

Serving size: 1 (2oz) patty

Nutrient analysis per serving: 123 calories, 17 gm protein, 4 gm carbohydrate, 4 gm fat, .75 gm fiber

Turkey Meatballs with Basil Cream Sauce

Festive tip:

Insert wooden skewers into each meatball. Top meatballs with a small basil leaf and serve on a white platter. Spoon cream sauce into a bowl and place in center of the serving platter.

8-10 whole wheat crackers, crushed
1 tsp basil
1 tsp salt
1 tsp pepper
1 lb extra lean ground turkey
½ cup finely chopped lean ham
½ cup grated Parmesan cheese

Basil Cream Sauce

½ cup low-fat mayonnaise
½ cup low-fat sour cream
¼ cup skim milk
2 tsp basil
½ tsp Splenda®

In a large bowl, combine the 1st 4 ingredients and mix well. Crumble turkey, ham, and cheese over cracker mixture and mix well. Shape into 25-30 meatballs. Place in a 9 x 13 baking dish coated with nonstick cooking spray. Bake @ 350° for 25-30 minutes or until no longer pink.

In a food processor, combine sauce ingredients and pulse until blended. Serve with meatballs.

Yield: ~14 servings

Serving size: 2 meatballs with ~1½ Tbsp sauce

Nutrient analysis per serving: 112 calories, 7.5 gm protein, 4 gm carbohydrate, 7.5 gm fat, .25 gm fiber

Vegetable Turkey Loaf

Festive tip:

Sprinkle oats onto white serving platter. Set turkey loaf on top of oats. Garnish platter with celery stalks, carrot sticks and fresh mushrooms.

¼ cup chopped onion
¼ cup chopped celery
¼ cup shredded carrots
¼ cup chopped fresh mushroom
1 tsp canola oil
1 egg
¼ cup oats, uncooked
½ cup frozen spinach, thawed and squeezed dry
¼ tsp garlic powder
¼ tsp thyme
¼ tsp seasoned salt
¼ tsp salt
¼ tsp pepper
1 lb extra lean ground turkey

In a medium skillet, sauté onion, celery, carrots, and mushroom in oil until tender. Remove from heat. In a medium bowl, combine egg, oats, spinach, sautéed vegetables, garlic powder, thyme, seasoned salt, salt, and pepper and mix well. Crumble turkey over egg mixture and mix well. Shape into a loaf and place in a 9 x 5 loaf pan. Bake @ 350° for 55-60 minutes or until meat thermometer reads 170°. Let stand for 5-10 minutes.

Yield: 8 servings

Serving size: 2 oz turkey loaf

Nutrient Analysis per serving: 134 calories, 11 gm protein, 5 gm carbohydrate, 7 gm fat, 1 gm fiber

*Good source of fiber

Cajun Turkey Tenderloin

Festive tip:

Slice turkey and serve over black beans, corn, and diced tomatoes. Garnish with a parsley sprig and lemon wedge.

2 Tbsp cider vinegar
1 Tbsp lemon juice
1 Tbsp canola oil
1 tsp paprika
½ tsp onion salt
½ tsp coarse ground pepper
¼ tsp garlic salt
⅛ tsp cayenne pepper
.75 lb skinless turkey breast tenderloins

In a large resealabe bag, combine the 1st 8 ingredients. Add turkey and refrigerate for 2-4 hours. Remove turkey and discard marinade. Grill turkey, covered, over med-hot coals for ~6-8 minutes on each side or until no longer pink.

Yield: 6 servings

Serving size: 2 oz turkey

Nutrient analysis per serving: 97 calories, 17 gm protein, 0 gm carbohydrate, 3 gm fat, 0 gm fiber

*Good source of healthy fat

Thanksgiving Turkey

Festive tip:

In a large saucepan, place 1 sliced pear, 1 sliced onion, 2 chopped celery stalks, and 1 cinnamon stick and cover with water. Bring to boil and simmer ~1 minute. Drain water. Place pear mixture inside turkey along with 4 thyme leaves and 4 sage leaves before baking.

1 (14-16 lb) frozen young turkey, thawed

Brine

1 cup sea salt
4 (15 oz) cans chicken broth
1 Tbsp black peppercorns
1 Tbsp rosemary
1 Tbsp marjoram
1 gallon ice water
¼ cup canola oil

In a Dutch oven, combine salt, broth, peppercorns, rosemary, and marjoram. Bring to a boil stirring often until salt dissolves. Remove from heat. Let cool to room temp.

In a 5 gallon bucket, combine broth mixture with ice water. Remove giblets and neck from turkey and clean well. Place clean turkey into bucket. Refrigerate at least 6 hours, turning turkey once during brining. Remove turkey and rinse well. Discard brine. Place turkey on a roasting rack in a large roasting pan. Pat dry with paper towels. Tuck wings back. Brush turkey with oil.

Roast turkey @ 450° for 30 minutes. Remove from oven, decrease temp to 350°. Cover turkey with a loose foil tent. Return turkey to oven and cook for 2-2½ hours or until meat thermometer reads 170° when inserted into the thickest part of the breast. Let rest, covered, for 15 minutes before carving.

Yield: ~128 servings

Serving size: 2 oz turkey

Nutrient analysis per serving: 118 calories, 16 gm protein, 0 carbohydrate, 5.5 gm fat, 0 gm fiber

Pecan-Crusted Shrimp

Festive tip:

Serve shrimp with cherry tomato halves, lemon slices and garnish with chives.

4 Tbsp olive oil, divided
1 Tbsp minced parsley
1 tsp lemon juice
1 tsp Splenda®
½ tsp salt
¼ tsp coconut extract
¼ cup chopped pecans
2 Tbsp self-rising cornmeal
1 egg, slightly beaten
2 Tbsp skim milk
½ lb uncooked med shrimp, peeled and deveined

In a small bowl, combine 2 Tbsp olive oil, parsley, lemon juice, Splenda®, salt, and coconut extract and mix well. Set aside. In a food processor, pulse pecans until finely ground. In a shallow bowl, combine pecans and cornmeal and mix well. In another small bowl, mix egg and milk.

In a large skillet, bring remaining oil to med-high heat. Dip shrimp into egg mixture and then into pecan mixture. Cook shrimp ~3-4 minutes on each side or until shrimp turns pink. Place shrimp on a lettuce-lined plate and drizzle with olive oil mixture.

Yield: 5 servings

Serving size: 3-4 shrimp

Nutrient analysis per serving: 208 calories, 12 gm protein, 4 gm carbohydrate, 16 gm fat, 1 gm fiber

*Good source of fiber and healthy fat

Apricot-Glazed Shrimp

¼ cup sugar-free apricot preserves
1 Tbsp soy sauce
1 Tbsp lemon juice
1 garlic clove, minced
½ lb uncooked med shrimp, peeled and deveined

Soak wooden skewers in water. In a small bowl, combine apricot preserves, soy sauce, lemon juice, and garlic and mix well. Set aside. Thread shrimp onto skewers and brush with apricot glaze. Grill shrimp over med-hot coals ~3 minutes on each side, brushing with additional glaze. Shrimp should turn pink before turning and taken off the grill. Serve immediately.

Yield: 4 servings

Serving size: 4-5 shrimp

Nutrient analysis per serving: 86 calories, 16 gm protein, 3 gm carbohydrate, 1 gm fat, 0 gm fiber

Shrimp Scampi

Festive tip:

Peel and cut two avocados in half, removing the seed. Fill each avocado half with shrimp and top with chopped tomato. Garnish with minced parsley.

2 garlic cloves, minced
4 Tbsp olive oil
1 lb uncooked med shrimp, peeled and deveined
¼ cup lemon juice
½ tsp salt
½ tsp pepper
¼ tsp seafood seasoning
Dash cayenne pepper
½ cup grated Parmesan cheese
1 Tbsp parsley

In a large skillet, sauté garlic in oil for 2-3 minutes. Add shrimp, lemon juice, salt, pepper, seafood seasoning, and cayenne pepper. Stir frequently until shrimp are pink and firm. Remove from heat and sprinkle with cheese and parsley.

Yield: 8 servings

Serving size: 4-5 shrimp

Nutrient analysis per serving: 122 calories, 17 gm protein, 2 gm carbohydrate, 5 gm fat, 0 gm fiber

*Good source of healthy fat

Pan-Seared Sea Scallops

Festive tip:

Serve scallops in center of a white platter. Take different vegetable purees, such as, pea, butternut squash, carrot, etc. and spoon a small amount of each around the scallops. Garnish with watercress.

2 Tbsp water
2 Tbsp rice vinegar
1½ Tbsp + 1½ tsp olive oil, divided
2 garlic cloves, minced
1 tsp salt
1 tsp pepper
1 tsp basil
1 lb sea scallops, cleaned
Lemon wedges

In a medium bowl, combine water, vinegar, 1½ tsp oil, garlic, salt, pepper, and basil and mix well. Add scallops; cover, and refrigerate for 30 minutes-1 hour.

In a large skillet, bring 1½ Tbsp oil to med-high heat. Discard marinade and cook scallops ~2-3 minutes on each side or until golden brown. Serve scallops on a lettuce-lined plate and garnish with lemon wedges.

Yield: 8 servings

Serving size: 2 oz sea scallops

Nutrient analysis per serving: 81 calories, 9.5 gm protein, 1.5 gm carbohydrate, 4 gm fat, 0 gm fiber

*Good source of healthy fat

Shrimp Lettuce Wraps

Festive tip:

Try other meats, seafood, poultry, vegetables and reduced-fat cheese combinations. Some ideas: tuna, caprese, Greek, egg, Cobb, Nicoise, or chicken salad OR fajita lettuce wraps.

¼ cup chopped peanuts
¼ cup of each chopped basil leaves, cilantro leaves, mint leaves
¼ cup soy sauce
¼ cup water
2 Tbsp lime juice
2 tsp Splenda®
½ tsp ground ginger
1 lb uncooked med shrimp, peeled and deveined
½ tsp salt
½ tsp pepper
2 Tbsp canola oil
2 garlic cloves, minced
2 carrots, peeled and shredded
4 scallions, chopped
1 small cucumber, peeled, seeded, and chopped
16 large lettuce leaves

In a medium bowl, combine peanuts, basil, cilantro, mint, soy sauce, water, lime juice, Splenda®, and ginger and mix well. Divide into 4 small dipping bowls.

Sprinkle shrimp with salt and pepper. In a large skillet, bring oil to med-high heat. Add garlic and shrimp; cook until shrimp turns pink. Place shrimp and vegetables on a serving platter.

To eat, place lettuce leaf in palm of hand. Spoon shrimp, vegetables, and sauce onto lettuce leaf and roll it up like a burrito (fold sides and roll it up).

Yield: 16 servings

Serving size: 1 lettuce leaf, 2-3 shrimp, ~2 Tbsp vegetables, and ~1 Tbsp sauce

Nutrient analysis per serving: 77 calories, 9 gm protein, 3 gm carbohydrate, 4 gm fat, 1 gm fiber

*Good source of fiber and healthy fat

Fish Tacos with Garlic Tartar Sauce

Festive tip:

Serve on a colorful plate with lime wedges and avocado slices.

1 lb tilapia
½ tsp salt
½ tsp pepper
1 Tbsp olive oil
2 Tbsp chopped green pepper
2 Tbsp chopped onion
1 garlic clove, minced
½ tsp cumin
½ tsp cilantro
2 Tbsp lime juice
4 (7") whole wheat tortillas, warmed

Garlic Tartar Sauce

¼ cup low-fat mayonnaise
1 garlic clove, minced
2 Tbsp capers
1 Tbsp lemon juice
½ tsp parsley
⅛ tsp salt

Sprinkle fish with salt and pepper and place in a 9 x 13 baking dish coated with nonstick cooking spray. Broil 4-6" from broiler for 4-6 minutes on each side. Once fish flakes easily, cut into 1" pieces.

In a large skillet, heat oil and sauté green pepper, onion, and garlic until tender. Add cumin and cilantro and mix well. Add fish to skillet and heat through. Stir in lime juice.

Cut tortillas in half. Fill ½ tortilla with fish mixture and fold over to make a taco.

For sauce: In a small bowl, combine all ingredients and mix well. Serve on top of fish taco.

Yield: 8 servings

Serving size: 2 oz fish, 1½ tsp vegetable, ½ tortilla, and 1 Tbsp sauce

Nutrient analysis per serving: 173 calories, 15 gm protein, 8 gm carbohydrate, 8 gm fat, 5 gm fiber

*Excellent source of fiber

Crab Salad Canapés

Festive tip:

Serve on a white
rectangle plate.
Garnish with
watercress cuttlings.

1 (6 oz) can crab meat, drained
4 oz light cream cheese
3 Tbsp low-fat mayonnaise
1 tsp chopped green onion
½ tsp lemon juice
¼ tsp garlic salt
¼ tsp seafood seasoning
1 small cucumber, cut into ¼" slices

In a medium bowl, combine the 1st 7 ingredients and mix well.
Spoon crab salad onto cucumber slices.

Yield: ~14 servings

Serving size: 2 canapés

Nutrient analysis per serving: 40 calories, 4 gm protein, 2 gm
carbohydrate, 2 gm fat, .5 gm fiber

Stuffed Sole with Dill Sauce

Festive tip:

Spoon dill sauce over a colorful plate and serve fish over sauce. Garnish with fresh blackberries and sprinkle fish with dill.

2 Tbsp chopped onion
2 Tbsp chopped celery
1 garlic clove, minced
2 tsp olive oil
½ cup chicken broth
¼ cup lemon juice
2 Tbsp shredded Parmesan cheese
¾ tsp parsley
1 (4 oz) can crab meat, drained
¼ tsp Creole seasoning
2 (6 oz) sole fillets
¼ tsp salt
¼ tsp pepper

Dill Sauce

¼ cup low-fat sour cream
1 Tbsp lemon juice
1½ tsp dill
⅛ tsp ground mustard
⅛ tsp garlic salt

In a small skillet, sauté onion, celery, and garlic in oil until tender. In a medium bowl, combine broth, lemon juice, sautéed vegetables, cheese, and parsley and mix well. Set aside. Spoon crab onto each sole fillet and sprinkle with Creole seasoning. Roll sole fillet up and secure with a toothpick. Place stuffed sole in a 1½ Qt baking dish and sprinkle with salt and pepper. Pour broth mixture over fish. Cover and bake @ 350° for ~25 minutes or until fish flakes easily.

For sauce: In a small bowl, combine all ingredients; mix well and serve with fish.

Yield: 6 servings

Serving size: 2 oz stuffed fish with ~1 Tbsp sauce

Nutrient analysis per serving: 158 calories, 18 gm protein, 4 gm carbohydrate, 8 gm fat, 0 gm fiber

Baked Tilapia with Cucumber Sauce

Festive tip:

Serve fish on a colorful plate and place a dollop of sauce on the side. Take a few thin slices of cucumber and fan them out, then place on top of sauce and garnish fish with parsley sprig.

¼ cup red wine vinegar
2 Tbsp water
1 Tbsp olive oil
½ tsp salt
½ tsp pepper
⅛ tsp garlic powder
2 (6 oz) tilapia fillets

Cucumber Sauce

½ cup diced cucumber
½ cup nonfat plain yogurt
¼ tsp dill
¼ tsp salt
⅛ tsp white pepper
⅛ tsp prepared horseradish

In a large resealable bag, combine the 1st 6 ingredients. Place tilapia in bag and refrigerate ~1 hour. Discard marinade. Place tilapia on a cookie sheet coated with nonstick cooking spray. Broil 4-6" from broiler for ~4-6 minutes on each side or until fish flakes easily.

For sauce: In a small bowl, combine all ingredients; mix well and serve with fish.

Yield: 6 servings

Serving size: 2 oz fish with ~2 Tbsp sauce

Nutrient analysis per serving: 113 calories, 15 gm protein, 2 gm carbohydrate, 4 gm fat, 0 gm fiber

*Good source of healthy fat

Balsamic-Glazed Salmon

2 (6 oz) salmon fillets
½ tsp salt, divided
¼ tsp pepper
2 Tbsp Splenda®
1 Tbsp cornstarch
½ tsp cracked pepper
⅛ tsp garlic powder
1 cup chicken broth
½ cup balsamic vinegar

Sprinkle salmon with ¼ tsp salt and pepper. In a small saucepan, combine Splenda®, cornstarch, cracked pepper, ¼ tsp salt, and garlic powder. Slowly add in broth and vinegar, and bring to boil over medium heat while stirring constantly. Simmer until thickened, ~20-25 minutes.

Brush salmon with glaze on all sides. Save remaining glaze to brush salmon while cooking and for festive tip, if desired. Broil salmon 4-6" from broiler for 4-6 minutes on each side or until fish flakes easily.

Yield: 6 servings

Serving size: 2 oz salmon

Nutrient analysis per serving: 119 calories, 12 gm protein, 4 gm carbohydrate, 6 gm fat, 0 gm fiber

Grilled Citrus Halibut

2 (6 oz) halibut steaks
½ tsp salt
½ tsp pepper
¼ cup red wine vinegar
1 Tbsp olive oil
1 Tbsp water
1 Tbsp lime juice
½ tsp parsley
¼ tsp orange zest
¼ tsp lemon zest

Sprinkle halibut with salt and pepper. In a small bowl, whisk together vinegar, oil, water, lime juice, parsley, orange and lemon zest until well blended. Brush halibut with a generous amount of marinade on all sides. Coat grill with nonstick cooking spray. Grill halibut over med-hot coals for 4-6 minutes on each side or until center is opaque. Brush with marinade often.

Yield: 6 servings

Serving size: 2 oz halibut

Nutrient analysis per serving: 87 calories, 12 gm protein, 0 gm carbohydrate, 5 gm fat, 0 gm fiber

*Good source of healthy fat

Tuna Steaks with Garlic Lime Sauce

Festive tip:

Serve tuna with steamed asparagus topped with pecans. Garnish with fresh raspberries.

¼ cup lime juice
2 Tbsp olive oil
2 (6 oz) tuna steaks
1 tsp chopped fresh cilantro
1 garlic clove, minced
½ tsp mustard seeds
½ tsp ground mustard
½ tsp salt
½ tsp coarse ground pepper
Fresh lime wedges and cilantro

Garlic Lime Sauce

1 garlic clove, minced
¼ cup lime juice
¼ cup soy sauce
1 tsp olive oil
½ tsp parsley

In a small bowl, combine lime juice and oil and mix well. Place tuna on a plate and brush with lime juice mixture. In a small bowl, combine cilantro, garlic, mustard seeds, mustard, salt, and pepper and mix well. Sprinkle cilantro mixture over steaks and press into flesh. Wrap in plastic and refrigerate for 4 hours.

Grill over med-hot coals for 4-5 minutes on each side or until tuna flakes easily. Garnish with lime wedges and cilantro, if desired.

For sauce: In a small bowl, combine sauce ingredients and mix well. Serve in condiment bowls with steak.

Yield: 6 servings

Serving size: 2 oz tuna with ~1 Tbsp sauce

Nutrient analysis per serving: 168 calories, 18 gm protein, 4 gm carbohydrate, 9 gm fat, .25 gm fiber

*Excellent source of healthy fat

Beef and Pork Bites

Lean Beef Chili
Spicy Meatball Stew
Swedish Meatballs
Hot Spaghetti Meat Sauce
Sloppy Joe Meat
Hamburger Tomato Skillet
Beef Stroganoff
Italian-Style Hamburger
Fiery Cheeseburger
Ricotta Cheese Meatloaf
Salisbury Steak
Shredded Beef
Beef Fajitas
Swiss Steak
Marinated Flank Steak
Green Chile Sirloin
Peppered Sirloin Steak
Garlic-Mustard Beef Tenderloin
Rosemary Veal Cutlets
Southwestern Pork Stew
Pork 'n' Pinto Beans
Barbeque Pork
Nutty Pork Bites
Pork Kabobs
Pork Medallions
Pork Stir-fry
Thyme Pork Chops
Pork Loin with Cilantro Sauce
Pork and Green Bean Casserole
Pork Chops with Apple Stuffing
Pork Asparagus Roll-Ups
Ham and Eggplant Parmesan
Herb-Crusted Pork Loin
Stuffed Pork Loin
Glazed Ham

My name is Alan and I had surgery in January 2006. I lost 120 lbs in 1 year and went from a size 56 to a size 36. Life has changed since having this surgery because I eat much smaller amounts and healthier foods.

I shop differently at the grocery store and avoid high sugar and high fat foods. In the past I would fry foods and I no longer prepare foods in an unhealthy way. At restaurants, I have found that I have to occupy my time. I will be with family or friends and because of the small amounts that I eat, I am finished before others. This has been something I have had to adjust to.

When food is brought to work, I will have a snack before going so that I am not starving. Many times there are fruit or vegetable trays and lean meats to choose from. I always take my own drink because I do not drink carbonation. That was difficult to give up and it seems to be found at potlucks very often. So I make sure I am prepared before going.

Lean Beef Chili

Festive tip:

Serve chili in a
bowl and set on a
plate with a side
of romaine lettuce
leaves topped
with orange and
grapefruit slices.
Garnish chili with
orange zest curls.

1 lb extra lean ground beef
1 garlic clove, minced
½ cup chopped onion
½ cup chopped green pepper
1 (10 oz) can diced tomatoes with green chiles
1 (14 oz) can chili beans, rinsed and drained
3 cups water
1 Tbsp chili powder
½ tsp garlic salt
½ tsp pepper

In a Dutch oven, cook ground beef with garlic, onion, and green
pepper until meat is no longer pink. Stir in tomatoes, beans,
water, chili powder, garlic salt, and pepper. Bring to boil; cover,
simmer for 30 minutes.

Yield: 16 servings

Serving size: ½ cup chili

Nutrient analysis per serving: 102 calories, 9.5 gm protein, 6 gm
carbohydrate, 5 gm fat, 1.5 gm fiber

*Good source of fiber

Spicy Meatball Stew

Festive tip:

Serve stew in a colorful bowl and set on a white plate with a side of a steamed squash. Top meatballs with sliced green onion and parsley.

1 egg
¼ cup whole wheat flour
1 garlic clove, minced
1 Tbsp chopped onion
¼ tsp salt
¼ tsp pepper
¼ tsp basil
¼ tsp rosemary
1 lb extra lean ground beef
2 tsp olive oil
1 (15 oz) can beef broth
1 (10.75 oz) can low-fat, reduced-sodium cream of mushroom soup, condensed
1 celery rib, chopped
1 small carrot, chopped
1 (10 oz) can diced tomatoes with green chiles, drained

In a large bowl, combine the 1st 8 ingredients and mix well. Add ground beef and mix well. Shape into 25-30 meatballs. In a Dutch oven, bring oil to med-high heat and cook meatballs ~5-7 minutes or until no longer pink. Drain. Stir in broth, soup, celery, carrot, and tomatoes. Bring to boil; cover, simmer 40-45 minutes or until vegetables are tender.

Yield: ~15 servings

Serving size: ½ cup stew

Nutrient analysis per serving: 113 calories, 9 gm protein, 4.5 gm carbohydrate, 6 gm fat, 1 gm fiber

*Good source of fiber

Swedish Meatballs

Festive tip:

Serve meatballs on a white plate with grilled zucchini, squash, and tomato kabobs.

1 egg
16-20 whole wheat crackers, crushed
½ tsp salt
½ tsp pepper
¼ tsp dried minced onion
1 lb extra lean ground beef
2 (10.75 oz) cans low-fat, reduced-sodium cream of mushroom soup, condensed
1 cup low-fat sour cream
1 cup skim milk
2 tsp paprika
1 tsp Worcestershire sauce

In a large bowl, combine the 1st 5 ingredients and mix well. Add ground beef and mix well. Form 25-30 meatballs. Place in a 9 x 13 baking dish coated with nonstick cooking spray. Bake @ 350° for 20-25 minutes. Drain any grease from pan.

In a large saucepan, heat soup, sour cream, milk, paprika, and Worcestershire sauce stirring until smooth. Pour sauce over meatballs and bake for an additional 30 minutes or until cooked through.

Yield: ~14 servings

Serving size: 2 meatballs with 4 Tbsp sauce

Nutrient analysis per serving: 161 calories, 10 gm protein, 8 gm carbohydrate, 9 gm fat, 1 gm fiber

*Good source of fiber

Hot Spaghetti Meat Sauce

Festive tip:

Serve meat sauce over mushrooms sautéed in a small amount of olive oil and garlic. Top with parmesan cheese and olives.

1 lb extra lean ground beef
½ cup chopped onion
1 garlic clove, minced
2½ cups tomato sauce
1 (4 oz) can diced green chiles, drained
1 Tbsp Worcestershire sauce
1 tsp chili powder
1 tsp salt
½ tsp pepper
Parmesan cheese
Sliced ripe olives

In a large skillet, cook ground beef, onion, and garlic until meat is no longer pink. Add tomato sauce, chiles, Worcestershire sauce, chili powder, salt, and pepper and stir well. Bring to boil; reduce heat, simmer 5-10 minutes. Serve in a bowl and top with Parmesan cheese and olives.

Yield: ~11 servings

Serving size: ½ cup meat sauce, 1 tsp Parmesan cheese, and 1 tsp olives

Nutrient analysis per serving: 141 calories, 12 gm protein, 6 gm carbohydrate, 8 gm fat, 1.25 gm fiber

*Good source of fiber

Sloppy Joe Meat

Festive tip:

Try variations of sloppy joe meat by adding ½ cup corn and 1 (4 oz) can of mushrooms or serve meat over ½ cup cooked whole wheat pasta.

Try making a sloppy joe meat casserole by adding ½ cup cooked whole wheat elbow macaroni, 1 cup kidney beans, (rinsed and drained), 1 (4 oz) can chopped green chiles. Then place in a 9 x 13 baking dish coated with nonstick cooking spray. Cover and bake @ 375° for 25 minutes or until bubbly. Uncover; sprinkle with 1 cup reduced-fat shredded cheese. Bake 5-8 minutes or until cheese is melted.

1 lb extra lean ground beef
½ cup chopped onion
½ cup chopped green pepper
1½ cups tomato sauce
3 Tbsp Splenda®
1 Tbsp tomato paste
1 Tbsp Worcestershire sauce
½ tsp pepper
¼ tsp salt
¼ tsp seasoned salt
Reduced-fat shredded cheese

In a large skillet, cook ground beef with onion and green pepper until meat is no longer pink. In a medium bowl, combine tomato sauce, Splenda®, tomato paste, Worcestershire sauce, pepper, salt, and seasoned salt and stir well. Add tomato sauce mixture to meat mixture and mix well. Heat through. Serve in a small bowl or place in a whole wheat tortilla and sprinkle with cheese.

Yield: 18 servings

Serving size: ¼-⅓ cup sloppy joe meat with 2 Tbsp cheese

Nutrient analysis per serving: 110 calories, 11 gm protein, 3 gm carbohydrate, 6 gm fat, .5 gm fiber

Hamburger Tomato Skillet

Festive tip:

Make stuffed green peppers with hamburger skillet. Cut the tops off of 4 green peppers and remove seeds and ribs. Steam peppers cut side down, on a rack in a pot with 1" boiling water, covered, for ~10 minutes. Place peppers in a 9 x 13 baking pan coated with nonstick cooking spray. Sprinkle with salt and pepper and fill with hamburger skillet. Bake, loosely covered with foil, @ 375° for ~20 minutes.

1 lb extra lean ground beef
1 (2 oz) package onion soup mix
1 (14 oz) can diced tomatoes
½ cup water
½ cup frozen corn
½ cup frozen green beans
½ cup frozen sliced okra

In a large skillet, cook ground beef until no longer pink. Add soup mix, tomatoes, and water to skillet and mix well. Stir in corn, green beans, and okra. Bring to boil; cover, and simmer 15 minutes or until vegetables are tender.

Yield: ~8 servings

Serving size: 2 oz meat with ¼-½ cup vegetables

Nutrient analysis per serving: 188 calories, 17 gm protein, 8 gm carbohydrate, 9 gm fat, 1 gm fiber

*Good source of fiber

Beef Stroganoff

Festive tip:

Serve beef stroganoff over a small portion of whole wheat noodles and surround entrée with tomato wedges.

1 lb flank steak, cut into 1" pieces
1 (10.75 oz) low-fat, reduced-sodium cream of mushroom soup, condensed
1 small onion, chopped
1 (4 oz) jar sliced mushrooms, drained
¼ cup water
2 Tbsp Worcestershire sauce
1 Tbsp tomato paste
1 garlic clove, minced
½ tsp salt
½ tsp pepper
½ tsp paprika
1 cup low-fat sour cream

In a 2.5 Qt crock pot, combine the 1st 11 ingredients and mix well. Cover and cook on low for 8 hours or until beef is tender. Add sour cream and mix well.

Yield: 8 servings

Serving size: 2 oz steak with 4 Tbsp soup mixture

Nutrient analysis per serving: 207 calories, 21 gm protein, 7 gm carbohydrate, 10 gm fat, 1 gm fiber

*Good source of fiber

Italian-Style Hamburger

Festive tip:

Serve patties on
a plate lined with
purple cabbage leaves
and a side of tomato
slices sprinkled with
Italian seasoning.

2-3 whole wheat crackers, crushed
¼ cup chopped onion
¼ cup chopped green pepper
½ tsp Italian seasoning
¼ tsp salt
¼ tsp pepper
⅛ tsp garlic powder
1 lb extra lean ground beef
1 Tbsp olive oil
4 slices reduced-fat cheese

In a large bowl, combine the 1st 7 ingredients and mix well. Add ground beef and mix well. Shape into 8 small patties. In a large skillet, bring oil to med-high heat. Cook patties for ~3 minutes on each side or until meat is no longer pink. Top each patty with ½ slice of cheese.

Yield: 8 servings

Serving size: 1 (2 oz) patty with ½ slice cheese

Nutrient analysis per serving: 214 calories, 18 gm protein, 4 gm carbohydrate, 13 gm fat, .25 gm fiber

Fiery Cheese Burger

Festive tip:

Make a hamburger salad. Place a hamburger patty on a bed of salad vegetables, mushrooms, and red onion slices. Top with avocado or black bean salsa.

¼ cup tomato salsa
2 Tbsp chopped onion
2 Tbsp canned, diced jalapenos
½ tsp garlic salt
½ tsp pepper
½ tsp cumin
½ tsp cilantro
1 lb extra lean ground beef
4 slices mozzarella cheese made with part skim milk
1 plum tomato, sliced
2 Tbsp sliced ripe olives

In a large bowl, combine the 1st 7 ingredients and mix well. Add ground beef and mix well. Shape into 8 small patties. Grill, covered, over med-hot coals for 7-8 minutes on each side or until no longer pink. Top each patty with ½ slice of cheese, tomato slice, and a few olive slices.

Yield: 8 servings

Serving size: 1 (2 oz) patty, ½ slice cheese, 1 tomato slice, and ~1 tsp olives

Nutrient analysis per serving: 189 calories, 18 gm protein, 2 gm carbohydrate, 12 gm fat, .5 gm fiber

Ricotta Cheese Meatloaf

Festive tip:

Make 12 individual meatloaves by pinching a small portion of meat, shaping into an oval, and placing in 12 cup muffin pan. Bake @ 375° for ~25 minutes. Let stand 5 minutes before serving. Top with pimentos and parsley sprigs.

½ cup skim milk Ricotta cheese
1 egg
3 Tbsp low carbohydrate or no added sugar ketchup
2 Tbsp chopped onion
2 Tbsp chopped green pepper
10 whole wheat crackers, crushed
½ tsp garlic salt
½ tsp pepper
1 lb extra lean ground beef

In a large bowl, combine the 1st 8 ingredients and mix well. Add ground beef and mix well. Press into a 9 x 5 loaf pan. Bake @ 375° for ~35 minutes or until meat thermometer reads 160-165°. Drain. Cook an additional 5 minutes. Let stand 10 minutes before serving.

*This recipe used Walden Farms® Calorie, Carb & Sugar Free Ketchup.

Yield: 12 servings

Serving size: ~1½ oz meatloaf

Nutrient analysis per serving: 168 calories, 16 gm protein, 3 gm carbohydrate, 9 gm fat, .5 gm fiber

Salisbury Steak

Festive tip:

Serve Salisbury steak on a colorful plate with a side of roasted vegetables. Garnish with star fruit slices and parsley sprig.

1 egg
10-12 whole wheat crackers, crushed
½ cup chopped onion
½ tsp salt
¼ tsp pepper
Dash allspice
1 lb extra lean ground beef
1 tsp canola oil
1 (10.75 oz) can low-fat, reduced-sodium cream of mushroom soup, condensed
⅓ cup water
2 Tbsp Worcestershire sauce
½ tsp ground mustard

In a large bowl, combine the 1st 6 ingredients and mix well. Add ground beef and mix well. Shape into 8 small patties. In a large skillet brushed with oil, brown patties over medium heat for 3-4 minutes on each side. Remove and keep warm. In same skillet, combine soup, water, Worcestershire sauce, and mustard and mix well. Bring to a boil. Return patties to skillet. Cover and simmer for 15 minutes or until meat is no longer pink. Serve gravy with patties.

Yield: 8 servings

Serving size: 1 (2 oz) patty with 2½ Tbsp gravy

Nutrient analysis per serving: 235 calories, 19 gm protein, 8 gm carbohydrate, 14 gm fat, 1 gm fiber

*Good source of fiber

Shredded Beef

3 lbs sirloin tip roast
1 tsp beef bouillon granules
1 small onion, chopped
1 celery stalk, chopped
1 garlic clove, minced
1 bay leaf
1 (10.75 oz) can beef mushroom soup, condensed
2 (14 oz) cans beef broth

Cut roast to fit into a 2.5 Qt crock pot. Sprinkle roast with bouillon granules. Add onion, celery, garlic, and bay leaf to crock pot. In a large bowl, combine soup and broth; mix well and pour over roast. Cover and cook on low heat ~6-8 hours or until tender.

Remove meat and shred by pulling it apart with two forks. May also shred in a food processor with short pulses. Serve with some of cooking juices.

Yield: 24 servings

Serving size: 2 oz beef with ~3 Tbsp soup

Nutrient analysis per serving: 114 calories, 18 gm protein, 1.5 gm carbohydrate, 3.5 gm fat, .25 gm fiber

Beef Fajitas

¼ cup lime juice
¼ cup balsamic vinegar
¼ cup water
3 Tbsp olive oil
1 tsp garlic salt
1 tsp pepper
1 tsp chili powder
¾ tsp cilantro
½ tsp cumin
½ tsp orange extract
1½ lbs top sirloin steak, trimmed of fat and sliced into 8" pieces
1 tsp canola oil
1 red bell pepper, sliced
1 small onion, sliced
6 (7") whole wheat tortillas
⅓ cup reduced-fat shredded cheddar cheese
Salsa
2 avocados, sliced
2 limes, sliced

In a large resealable bag, combine the 1st 10 ingredients. Add steak and refrigerate ~4 hours. Discard marinade. In a large skillet brushed with oil, cook steak over med-high heat for ~4 minutes on each side. Remove steak and keep warm. Add red pepper and onion to skillet and cook 7-8 minutes or until tender. Place meat and vegetables on a heated tortilla and top with cheese, salsa, avocado, and lime juice squeezed from lime slices.

Yield: 12 servings

Serving size: 2 oz meat, ½ tortilla, ¼ cup vegetables, 1-2 avocado slices, and ~1 tsp cheese

Nutrient analysis per serving: 265 calories, 22 gm protein, 14 gm carbohydrate, 13 gm fat, 5 gm fiber

*Excellent source of fiber and healthy fat

Swiss Steak

Festive tip:

Serve steak with ¼ cup cooked spinach mixed with ¼ cup brown rice topped with shredded Swiss cheese.

1 Tbsp whole wheat flour
¼ tsp salt
¼ tsp pepper
⅛ tsp paprika
¾ lb sirloin steak
1 Tbsp canola oil
⅓ cup chopped onion
2 Tbsp chopped green pepper
1 garlic clove, minced
1 (15 oz) can beef broth
1 (14 oz) can diced tomatoes, drained

In a shallow bowl, combine flour, salt, pepper, and paprika and mix well. Coat steak with flour mixture. In a Dutch oven, bring oil to med-high heat and cook steak ~2 minutes on each side. Remove steak and keep warm. In the Dutch oven, sauté onion, green pepper, and garlic ~1-2 minutes. Add broth and tomatoes and stir well. Add steak; cover, and simmer for 2 hours or until steak is tender. Serve steak topped with tomatoes, onion, and green pepper.

Yield: ~6 servings

Serving size: 2 oz steak with ¼ cup vegetables and sauce

Nutrient analysis per serving: 160 calories, 19 gm protein, 5 gm carbohydrate, 6.5 gm fat, .5 gm fiber

*Good source of healthy fat

Marinated Flank Steak

Festive tip:

Serve steak on a
lettuce-lined plate.
Garnish steak with
capers and cherry
tomatoes.

¼ cup red wine vinegar
¼ cup capers
2 Tbsp lemon juice
2 Tbsp olive oil
2 Tbsp water
1 garlic clove, minced
1 tsp ground ginger
½ tsp salt
½ tsp cracked pepper
¾ lb flank steak

In a large resealable bag, combine the 1st 9 ingredients. Add steak
and refrigerate ~6-12 hours.

Remove steak and pour marinade into a small saucepan. Bring
to boil; cover, and simmer ~10 minutes. Grill steak over med-hot
coals for 6-7 minutes on each side for medium cooked steak.
Cut steak diagonal against the grain into thin slices. Serve with
sauce.

Yield: 6 servings

Serving size: 2 oz steak with ~1 Tbsp sauce

Nutrient analysis per serving: 176 calories, 20 gm protein, 1 gm
carbohydrate, 10 gm fat, .25 gm fiber

*Good source of healthy fat

Green Chile Sirloin

Festive tip:

Serve steak with sliced tomatillos sprinkled with lime juice and hot pepper flakes. Garnish with cilantro.

¼ cup white vinegar
½ cup beef broth
1 Tbsp canola oil
1 garlic clove, minced
2 tsp chili powder
1 tsp cumin
½ tsp salt
¼ tsp pepper
¾ lb top sirloin steak
½ small onion, sliced
1 (4 oz) can green chiles, drained

In a large resealable bag, combine the 1st 8 ingredients. Add steak and refrigerate 4-6 hours. Pour marinade into a medium skillet, bring to boil, and reduce to med-high heat for 10 minutes. Add onion and green chiles to skillet and cook until tender. Grill steak over med-hot coals for 6-7 minutes on each side for medium cooked steak. Top steak with onion and green chiles.

Yield: 6 servings

Serving size: 2 oz steak with 2 Tbsp sauce, onion, and green chiles

Nutrient analysis per serving: 159 calories, 16 gm protein, 3 gm carbohydrate, 9 gm fat, 1 gm fiber

*Good source of fiber and healthy fat

Peppered Sirloin Steak

Festive tip:

Spoon sauce onto a white plate. Place 5 steamed asparagus in a row on top of sauce. Serve steak on top of asparagus. Garnish plate with rosemary sprig.

½ cup chopped mushroom
½ cup chopped onion
1 garlic clove, minced
4 tsp canola oil, divided
2 (6 oz) sirloin steaks
1 tsp coarse ground black pepper
½ tsp salt
1 (15 oz) can beef broth
2 Tbsp soy sauce
¼ tsp Splenda®
2 Tbsp cornstarch
½ cup water

In a large skillet, heat 2 tsp oil and sauté mushroom, onion, and garlic until tender. Remove from skillet and keep warm. Sprinkle steaks with pepper and salt and press into steaks on both sides. Cook steaks in remaining oil until browned. Remove from skillet and keep warm. Add broth, soy sauce, and Splenda® to skillet and stir well. Return steaks and vegetables to skillet. Bring to boil; cover, and simmer for 35-40 minutes. Remove steaks. Dissolve cornstarch in water. Add to skillet and cook stirring constantly until thickened, ~2 minutes. Serve steaks with sauce.

Yield: 6 serving

Serving size: 2 oz steak with 4-5 Tbsp sauce

Nutrient analysis per serving: 160 calories, 19 gm protein, 5 gm carbohydrate, 7 gm fat, .5 gm fiber

*Good source of healthy fat

Garlic-Mustard Beef Tenderloin

2 (6 oz) beef tenderloin steaks
2 tsp Worcestershire sauce
¼ tsp salt
¼ tsp pepper
¼ cup whole grain mustard
¼ cup Dijon mustard
3 garlic cloves, minced
2 Tbsp red wine vinegar
2 tsp olive oil
1 tsp marjoram
Finely chopped chives

Place steaks on a plate and brush with Worcestershire sauce and sprinkle with salt and pepper. Set aside. In a small bowl, combine mustards, garlic, vinegar, oil, and marjoram and mix well.

Place steaks in a 1 Qt baking dish and pour ½ of sauce over meat, turn to coat. Cover and refrigerate for 1 hour. Grill steak over med-hot coals brushing with remaining sauce for 4-6 minutes on each side or until golden brown. Sprinkle with chives before serving.

Yield: 6 servings

Serving size: 2 oz steak

Nutrient analysis per serving: 152 calories, 17 gm protein, .5 gm carbohydrate, 8 gm fat, 0 gm fiber

Rosemary Veal Cutlets

Festive tip:

Serve veal on a
colorful plate with
a side of black-eyed
peas. Garnish veal
with grape tomatoes.

2 Tbsp olive oil, divided
2 Tbsp balsamic vinegar
2 Tbsp water
1 garlic clove, minced
½ tsp rosemary
½ tsp salt
½ tsp pepper
¾ lb veal loin chops, trimmed of visible fat
1 cup beef broth

In a large resealable bag, combine 1 Tbsp oil, vinegar, water, garlic, rosemary, salt, and pepper. Add veal and refrigerate 2-4 hours. Drain marinade into a small saucepan, add broth, and bring to boil. Reduce to med-high heat for ~10 minutes.

In a large skillet, bring remaining oil to med-high heat. Cook veal 3-4 minutes on each side. Add sauce to skillet. Bring to boil; cover, and simmer for 30 minutes or until tender.

Yield: 6 servings

Serving size: 2 oz veal with 3 Tbsp sauce

Nutrient analysis per serving: 153 calories, 19 gm protein, 0 gm carbohydrate, 8 gm fat, 0 gm fiber

*Good source of healthy fat

Southwestern Pork Stew

Festive tip:

Serve in a colorful bowl. Add a dollop of fat-free sour cream and garnish with minced cilantro.

1 lb pork loin chops, cut into 1" pieces
2 tsp olive oil
¼ cup chopped onion
1 celery stalk, chopped
1 garlic clove, minced
1 (15 oz) can chicken broth
1 (14 oz) can black beans, rinsed and drained
1 (10 oz) can diced tomatoes with green chiles
½ cup frozen corn
½ tsp cumin
½ tsp cilantro
½ tsp chili powder
½ tsp salt

In a Dutch oven, cook pork in oil with onion, celery, and garlic until no longer pink. Stir in remaining ingredients. Bring to boil; cover, simmer for 1 hour.

Yield: 8 servings

Serving size: ½ cup stew

Nutrient analysis per serving: 94 calories, 11 gm protein, 5.5 gm carbohydrate, 3 gm fat, 2 gm fiber

*Great source of fiber

Pork 'n' Pinto Beans

Festive tip:

Serve pork and pinto beans in lettuce-lined bowls. Garnish with cilantro.

1 lb dried pinto beans
3 lbs pork loin roast, trimmed and halved
1 tsp garlic salt
1 tsp pepper
1 (10 oz) can diced tomatoes with green chiles
1 small onion, chopped
¼ cup chili powder
½ tsp cumin
½ tsp cilantro
1 (15 oz) can chicken broth
Water

Place beans in a large pot and fill with water to cover beans by 2". Bring to boil and boil for 2 minutes. Remove from heat; cover, and let stand for 1 hour. Rinse and drain beans.

Place roast in a 6 Qt crock pot. Sprinkle roast with salt and pepper. In a large bowl, combine tomatoes, onion, chili powder, cumin, cilantro, and beans and mix well. Spoon over roast. Add broth and water to cover meat completely. Cover and cook on low for 8 hours. Remove meat and shred with 2 forks. Return shredded meat to crock pot.

Yield: 24 servings

Serving size: 2 oz pork with 2 Tbsp beans

Nutrient analysis per serving: 149 calories, 19 gm protein, 7 gm carbohydrate, 5 gm fat, 2.5 gm fiber

*Great source of fiber

Barbeque Pork

Festive tip:

Ideal uses for leftover pork loin roast: Fill in whole wheat pita bread along with romaine lettuce and tomato and top with low calorie dressing. OR make a wrap with whole wheat tortilla, pork loin roast, lettuce, tomato, cucumber slices, and sunflower seeds. Top with low calorie dressing, sour cream or mayo. OR add to salad greens and top with pineapple chunks and fat-free vinaigrette.

3 lbs pork loin roast, trimmed and halved
1 tsp salt
1 tsp pepper
2 (15 oz) cans tomato sauce
3 cups water
1 small onion, chopped
2 garlic cloves, minced
¼ cup prepared mustard
¼ cup Splenda®
¼ cup white vinegar
2 Tbsp Worcestershire sauce
2 tsp paprika
1 tsp pepper
½ tsp hot pepper sauce
Pinch ground cinnamon

Place roast in a 6 Qt crock pot and sprinkle with salt and pepper. In a large bowl, combine remaining ingredients; mix well and add to crock pot. Cover and cook on low for 8 hours.

Yield: 24 servings

Serving size: 2 oz pork with 5 Tbsp barbeque sauce

Nutrient analysis per serving: 136 calories, 17 gm protein, 4 gm carbohydrate, 6 gm fat, 1 gm fiber

*Good source of fiber

Nutty Pork Bites

Festive tip:

Place pork bites on a serving platter. Insert rosemary sprig in top of each pork bite instead of using ordinary toothpicks.

1 egg
8-10 whole wheat crackers, crushed
⅓ cup chopped almonds, toasted
2 tsp Worcestershire sauce
1 tsp parsley
1 tsp salt
⅛ tsp cayenne pepper
1 lb lean ground pork
1 cup water
1 (2 oz) package onion soup mix

In a large bowl, combine the 1st 7 ingredients and mix well. Add pork and mix well. Shape into 24-30 meatballs. In a large skillet, brown meatballs; drain. Place meatballs in a 9 x 13 baking dish coated with nonstick cooking spray.

In a small saucepan, combine water and soup mix. Bring to boil, stirring constantly until thickened, ~2 minutes. Pour over meatballs. Bake, covered, @ 350° for 35 minutes; then bake, uncovered, for 25-30 minutes or until cooked through.

Yield: ~14 servings

Serving size: 2 meatballs

Nutrient analysis per serving: 150 calories, 10 gm protein, 4 gm carbohydrate, 10 gm fat, 1 gm fiber

*Good source of fiber and healthy fat

Pork Kabobs

1.5 lbs pork tenderloin, cut into 1" pieces
1 small onion, quartered
1-2 tomatoes, quartered
1-2 large green peppers, quartered
1 large zucchini, cut into 1" slices
2 cups prepared sugar-free pineapple or orange drink
½ cup cider vinegar
¼ cup soy sauce
2 Tbsp canola oil
¼ tsp ground ginger
¼ tsp garlic salt
½ tsp salt
½ tsp pepper

Soak wooden skewers in water. Thread pork and vegetables onto skewers and place kabobs in a 15 x 11 baking dish. In a large bowl, combine pineapple or orange drink, vinegar, soy sauce, oil, ginger, and garlic salt and mix well. Pour over kabobs; cover, and refrigerate 4-6 hours, turning once.

Drain and discard marinade. Sprinkle kabobs with salt and pepper. Grill, covered, over med-hot coals for 6-8 minutes on both sides or until pork is cooked through.

Yield: ~12 servings

Serving size: 1 small kabob

Nutrient analysis per serving: 133 calories, 18 gm protein, 4.5 gm carbohydrate, 4.5 gm fat, 1 gm fiber

*Good source of fiber and healthy fat

Pork Medallions

Festive tip:

Serve medallions on a white plate. Spoon mango salsa over medallions and serve with a side of steamed asparagus.

1.2 lbs pork tenderloin, sliced into 1" medallions
½ tsp salt
½ tsp pepper
3 tsp canola oil, divided
½ cup diced mushrooms
1 (15 oz) can beef broth
¾ cup water
½ tsp fennel seeds
⅛ tsp garlic powder
2 Tbsp cornstarch

Sprinkle pork with salt and pepper. In a large skillet, bring 2 tsp oil to med-high heat. Cook pork ~6-8 minutes on each side or until cooked through. Remove pork and keep warm. In same skillet, heat remaining oil and sauté mushrooms until tender.

In a large bowl, combine broth, water, fennel seeds, garlic powder, and cornstarch and mix well. Pour into skillet. Bring to boil over medium heat, stirring constantly until thickened. Add pork; cover, and simmer 10-15 minutes. Serve pork with mushroom sauce.

Yield: 10 servings

Serving size: 2 oz pork with 3 Tbsp mushroom sauce

Nutrient analysis per serving: 111 calories, 16 gm protein, 1.5 gm carbohydrate, 4 gm fat, 0 gm fiber

Pork Stir-Fry

Festive tip:

Serve stir-fry on a square plate lined with snow peas. Sprinkle with boiled edamome.

1 lb pork loin chops, cut into 1" pieces
½ tsp salt
½ tsp pepper
4 tsp canola oil, divided
1 red pepper, sliced
2 small carrots, julienned
½ red onion, thinly sliced
1 Tbsp almonds
½ cup soy sauce
¼ cup water
1 Tbsp Splenda®
1 Tbsp cornstarch
¼ tsp ground ginger
¼ tsp garlic powder
⅛ tsp orange zest
⅛ tsp red pepper flakes, optional

Sprinkle pork with salt and pepper. In a large skillet, bring 2 tsp oil to med-high heat and cook pork until no longer pink. Remove and keep warm. In same skillet, sauté red pepper, carrots, onion, and almonds in remaining oil until crisp tender. Remove and keep warm.

In a medium bowl, combine remaining ingredients and mix well. Add to skillet and bring to boil. Return pork and vegetables to skillet and stir well. Heat through.

Yield: 8 servings

Serving size: 2 oz pork, ¼ cup vegetables, and 1-2 Tbsp sauce

Nutrient analysis per serving: 165 calories, 17 gm protein, 6 gm carbohydrate, 8 gm fat, 1 gm fiber

*Good source of fiber and healthy fat

Thyme Pork Chops

Festive tip:

Serve pork on a colorful plate and drizzle sauce around pork chops. Garnish with fresh thyme and tomato slices.

2 (4 oz) pork loin chops
½ tsp salt
½ tsp pepper
1 Tbsp canola oil
1 cup chicken broth
1 tsp thyme
2 tsp cornstarch

Sprinkle pork with salt and pepper. In a large skillet, bring oil to med-high heat and cook pork 3-4 minutes on each side or until no longer pink. In a small bowl, combine broth and thyme; mix well and pour into skillet. Bring to boil; cover, and simmer 15 minutes. Remove pork chops and keep warm.

Add cornstarch to skillet and bring to boil over medium heat, stirring constantly until thickened. Serve over pork chops.

Yield: 4 servings

Serving size: 2 oz pork with 2-3 Tbsp sauce

Nutrient analysis per serving: 157 calories, 17 gm protein, 2 gm carbohydrate, 8 gm fat, 0 gm fiber

*Good source of healthy fat

Pork Loin with Cilantro Sauce

Festive tip:

Serve pork over a small amount of fat-free refried beans spread onto a colorful plate. Spoon cilantro sauce over pork and garnish with fresh cilantro and tomato slices.

1 lb pork loin chops
½ tsp salt
½ tsp pepper
4 Tbsp lime juice + 1½ tsp, divided
¼ cup water
2 Tbsp olive oil
1 Tbsp hot pepper sauce
1 garlic clove, minced

Cilantro Sauce

½ cup nonfat plain yogurt
¼ cup low-fat sour cream
2-3 Tbsp fresh cilantro leaves
1 tsp serrano pepper, seeded and chopped
¼-½ tsp garlic salt

Sprinkle pork with salt and pepper. In a large resealable bag, combine 3 Tbsp lime juice, water, oil, hot pepper sauce, and garlic. Add pork to bag and refrigerate 2-4 hours.

In a food processor, combine yogurt, sour cream, cilantro, remaining lime juice, serrano pepper, and garlic salt. Pulse until smooth.

Remove pork and discard marinade. Grill pork over med-hot coals, covered, ~6-7 minutes on each side or until no longer pink. Serve with cilantro sauce.

Yield: 8 servings

Serving size: 2 oz pork with 1-2 Tbsp cilantro sauce

Nutrient analysis per serving: 158 calories, 19 gm protein, 3 gm carbohydrate, 8 gm fat, 0 gm fiber

Pork and Green Bean Casserole

Festive tip:

Slice several purple onion rings and place on top of casserole. Garnish with rosemary sprigs.

2 (4 oz) pork loin chops
½ tsp salt
½ tsp cracked pepper
1 Tbsp canola oil
½ cup chopped onion
1 (10.75 oz) can low-fat, reduced-sodium cream of mushroom soup, condensed
1 cup skim milk
1 cup frozen green beans, thawed

Sprinkle pork with salt and pepper. In a large skillet, bring oil to med-high heat and cook pork 3-4 minutes on each side or until browned. Place pork in a 9 x 13 baking dish coated with nonstick cooking spray.

In same skillet, sauté onion for 1 minute, then add remaining ingredients and mix well. Heat through. Pour soup mixture over pork. Cook, covered for 30 minutes @ 375°, then uncovered for 10-15 minutes.

Yield: 4 servings

Serving size: 2 oz pork with 6 Tbsp soup and green beans

Nutrient analysis per serving: 216 calories, 18 gm protein, 13 gm carbohydrate, 10 gm fat, 1.5 gm fiber

*Good source of fiber and healthy fat

Pork Chops with Apple Stuffing

Festive tip:

Serve pork and apple stuffing on a white plate with steamed asparagus. Garnish with parsley sprigs and whole walnuts.

1 lb pork loin chops
½ tsp salt
½ tsp pepper
1 Tbsp canola oil

Apple Stuffing

1 apple, cored and chopped
1 celery stalk, chopped
3 Tbsp chopped walnuts
3 Tbsp water
2 Tbsp chopped onion
¼ tsp salt
¼ tsp marjoram
⅛ tsp pepper
2 tsp Splenda®

Sprinkle pork with salt and pepper. In a large skillet, bring oil to med-high heat and cook pork ~2-3 minutes on each side. Place in a 9 x 13 baking dish.

In a large bowl, combine apple, celery, walnuts, water, onion, salt, marjoram, and pepper and toss gently. Spoon apple stuffing over pork chops and sprinkle with Splenda®. Cover and bake @ 350° for 1 hour or until meat is no longer pink.

Yield: 8 servings

Serving size: 2 oz pork with ~2 Tbsp stuffing

Nutrient analysis per serving: 136 calories, 17 gm protein, 3 gm carbohydrate, 6 gm fat, .75 gm fiber

*Good source of healthy fat

Pork Asparagus Roll-ups

Festive tip:

Serve on a colorful plate with orange slices and grapes. For a festive table setting, use light green table cloth and red napkins.

2 (4 oz) pork loin chops
2 tsp Dijon mustard
6 fresh asparagus spears, cleaned and trimmed
4 Tbsp shredded mozzarella cheese made with part skim milk
1 tsp parsley
½ tsp salt
½ tsp pepper
1 Tbsp olive oil
½ cup chicken broth
2 Tbsp hot water

Pound pork chops, with a meat tenderizer mallet, to the length of asparagus. Spread 1 tsp of mustard over each pork chop. Place 3 asparagus spears toward one edge of pork chop. Sprinkle each pork chop with 2 Tbsp cheese and ½ tsp parsley. Roll up pork to enclose asparagus. Fasten with skewers or toothpicks. Sprinkle with salt and pepper.

In an oven-proof skillet, bring oil to med-high heat and brown pork rolls ~3 minutes on each side. Pour broth over pork. Bake @ 350° for 20 minutes or until pork is no longer pink. Cut pork rolls in ½. Add water to remaining juices in pan and serve with pork rolls.

Yield: 4 servings

Serving size: ½ pork roll-up with 1-2 Tbsp broth

Nutrient analysis per serving: 153 calories, 19 gm protein, 1 gm carbohydrate, 7 gm fat, .5 gm fiber

*Good source of healthy fat

Ham and Eggplant Parmesan

Festive tip:

Spoon tomato sauce over white plate and set ham and eggplant parmesan slice on top of sauce. Sprinkle with parmesan cheese and olives. Garnish with fresh oregano leaves.

2 eggs
18 whole wheat crackers, crushed
1 Tbsp natural flavored protein powder
½ tsp salt
½ tsp pepper
½ tsp Italian seasoning
1 small eggplant, peeled and sliced into 6 slices, ~ ¼" thick
6 slices Prosciutto ham
6 mozzarella cheese slices made with part skim milk
1 (15 oz) can tomato sauce
2 tsp oregano
¼ tsp garlic salt
2 Tbsp grated Parmesan cheese, divided
1 Tbsp diced ripe olives, divided

In a shallow bowl, beat eggs. In another shallow bowl, combine cracker crumbs, protein powder, salt, pepper, and Italian seasoning and mix well. Dip eggplant slices into egg and then into cracker crumb mixture. Place in a 9 x 13 baking dish coated with nonstick cooking spray. Bake @ 350° for 30 minutes. Top with ham and cheese slices, and bake an additional 5 minutes.

In a small saucepan, bring tomato sauce, oregano, and garlic salt to a boil. Serve over eggplant, sprinkle with Parmesan cheese, and top with olives.

Yield: 6 servings

Serving size: 1 ham and eggplant parmesan, ¼ cup tomato sauce, 1 tsp Parmesan cheese, and ½ tsp olives

Nutrient analysis per serving: 202 calories, 22 gm protein, 18 gm carbohydrate, 5 gm fat, 3.25 gm fiber

*Excellent source of fiber

Herb-Crusted Pork Loin

Festive tip:

Serve pork on a white platter. Garnish with orange slices, cherry tomatoes, and basil leaves.

8-10 whole wheat crackers, crushed
½ tsp thyme
½ tsp garlic salt
½ tsp pepper
¼ tsp marjoram
¼ tsp basil
¼ cup Dijon mustard
1.2 lbs pork loin

In a small bowl, combine cracker crumbs, thyme, garlic salt, pepper, marjoram, and basil and mix well. Brush all sides of pork with mustard and sprinkle with crumb mixture. Place pork on a roasting rack in a roasting pan and bake, uncovered, @ 350° for 60-65 minutes or until meat thermometer reads 160-165°. Let stand 5 minutes and slice before serving.

Yield: ~10 servings

Serving size: 2 oz pork

Nutrient analysis per serving: 135 calories, 17 gm protein, 3 gm carbohydrate, 5 gm fat, .5 gm fiber

Stuffed Pork Loin

Festive tip:

Place pork on a wooden serving platter. Garnish with rosemary sprigs on each side of pork.

1.2 lbs pork loin
1 Tbsp + 3 tsp canola oil, divided
2 oz deli ham
2 oz sliced Swiss cheese
½ tsp ground mustard
½ tsp salt
½ tsp cracked pepper

Cut pork loin horizontally and lay flat. Flatten with meat tenderizer mallet. Brush with 1 Tbsp oil and layer with ham and cheese. Sprinkle with mustard, roll up meat, and tie with kitchen string. Place on a roasting rack in a roasting pan. Brush with 2 tsp oil and sprinkle with salt and pepper. Bake @ 350° for 60-65 minutes or until meat thermometer reads 160-165°. Brush with remaining oil occasionally while baking. Let stand 5 minutes. Slice before serving.

Yield: ~10 servings

Serving size: 2 oz pork

Nutrient analysis per serving: 182 calories, 22 gm protein, .5 gm carbohydrate, 9 gm fat, 0 gm fiber

Glazed Ham

5 lbs fully cooked whole boneless ham
½ cup sugar-free orange marmalade
¼ cup Dijon mustard
1 tsp rosemary
½ tsp garlic powder
½ tsp maple extract

Place ham on a roasting rack in a roasting pan. Bake @ 325° for 60-80 minutes or until meat thermometer reads 160°.

In a small saucepan, combine remaining ingredients. Heat through, stirring often. Brush ham with glaze. Bake an additional 20-30 minutes, brushing with glaze occasionally.

Yield: 40 servings

Serving size: 2 oz ham

Nutrient analysis per serving: 82 calories, 10 gm protein, 2 gm carbohydrate, 3.5 gm fat, 0 gm fiber

Salad and Salsa Bites

Chicken Caesar Salad
Sesame Chicken Salad
Chicken Kabob Salad
Mango Chicken Salad
Taco Salad
Citrus Shrimp Salad
Salmon Salad
Edamome Salad
Mardi Gras Bean Salad
Insalata Caprese Salad
Cottage Cheese Spinach Salad
Greek Salad
Strawberry Spinach Salad
Fruit Salad
Thousand Island Salad Dressing
French Salad Dressing
Raspberry-Sesame Vinaigrette
Lemon-Caper Vinaigrette
Poppy Seed Vinaigrette
Horseradish Sauce
Mango-Pineapple Salsa
Avocado Salsa
Berry Salsa
Black Bean Salsa
Chile-Citrus Salsa

We are Bill and Lisa of Carlsbad, NM. Bill's surgery was February, 2007, and Lisa's surgery was two months later in April. Bill has lost 160 pounds and Lisa has lost 120 pounds. It was very important to find a bariatric surgeon that stressed nutrition.

Together we learned how to adapt to this new relationship with food by making healthy choices, developing creative menus for the family at home, as well as sharing meals when eating out. We still enjoy cooking the same amount of food for meals as before surgery however now we freeze leftovers in 'our portion' sized amounts that Bill can easily take to work. Before surgery our favorite past time each night was enjoying a bowl of ice cream in bed while watching TV. We now enjoy an evening snack, such as sugar free pudding.

We feel one of the keys to our success is the mutual support we have given each other. We still attend social gatherings as a couple. We always carry with us our own sugar free drink mix packets to add to water in place of carbonated beverages. As a backup, we also carry simple snacks, such as peanuts or protein bars, with us where ever we go. For potlucks, we now have plenty of recipes to choose from and even non-WLS friends enjoy them. A cookbook written by a nutritionist specializing in bariatric diets is so needed and welcomed by WLS patients for each stage of their journey.

Chicken Caesar Salad

Festive tip:

Serve on a colorful square plate and garnish with tomato wedges and 2-3 scallions.

2 (6 oz) skinless chicken breasts, cut into strips
1 cup fat-free Italian salad dressing
¼ cup low-fat mayonnaise
2 Tbsp olive oil
2 Tbsp shredded Parmesan cheese
1 Tbsp lemon juice
1 tsp Dijon mustard
¾ tsp Worcestershire sauce
¼ tsp garlic powder
4 cups romaine lettuce
Fresh ground pepper

In a large resealable bag, marinade chicken in salad dressing for 1-2 hours

Discard marinade. Heat skillet and cook chicken over med-high heat for 3-4 minutes on each side or until no longer pink. Remove from heat and keep warm.

In a large bowl, combine mayonnaise, oil, cheese, lemon juice, mustard, Worcestershire sauce, and garlic powder and mix well. Add romaine lettuce and toss to coat. Top with chicken and sprinkle with pepper.

Yield: 6 servings

Serving size: 2 oz chicken with ⅔ cup salad

Nutrient analysis per serving: 185 calories, 19 gm protein, 7 gm carbohydrate, 9 gm fat, 1.25 gm fiber

*Good source of fiber and healthy fat

Sesame Chicken Salad

Festive tip:

Serve salad with
a side of fresh
raspberries and
sugar-free whipped
topping.

3 cups torn spinach leaves
7-8 cherry tomatoes, halved
1 Tbsp balsamic vinegar
½ tsp tarragon
¼ tsp salt
¼ tsp pepper
2 Tbsp olive oil
4 avocado slices, cubed
2 tsp lemon juice
2 (6 oz) skinless chicken breasts, grilled and cut into strips
3 Tbsp sesame seeds, toasted

In a large bowl, combine spinach and tomatoes. In a small bowl, whisk together vinegar, tarragon, salt, and pepper. Gradually whisk in oil until emulsified.

Toss together spinach, tomatoes, and olive oil dressing. In a medium bowl, toss avocado in lemon juice. Top spinach salad with chicken and avocados. Sprinkle with sesame seeds. Serve immediately.

Yield: 6 servings

Serving size: 2 oz chicken with ½ cup salad

Nutrient analysis per serving: 193 calories, 19 gm protein, 4 gm carbohydrate, 11.5 gm fat, 3 gm fiber

*Excellent source of fiber and healthy fat

Chicken Kabob Salad

Festive tip:

Use curved skewers
and serve kabob
salad on a square
plate.

1 lb skinless chicken breasts, cut into 1" pieces
1 small red pepper, cut into wedges
½ onion, cut into wedges
1 (8 oz) can pineapple chunks in its own juice, drained
½ cup soy sauce
2 Tbsp lemon juice
2 Tbsp Splenda®
1 Tbsp olive oil
¼ tsp garlic salt
¼ tsp pepper
4 cups romaine lettuce
2 Tbsp chopped green onion

Soak wooden skewers in water. Thread chicken, red pepper, onion, and pineapple onto skewers. In a small bowl, combine soy sauce, lemon juice, Splenda®, oil, garlic salt, and pepper and mix well.

Grill kabobs over med-hot coals ~10-15 minutes or until chicken is no longer pink. Turn and brush with soy sauce mixture frequently.

Combine lettuce and green onion. Place kabobs over salad and drizzle with remaining sauce.

Yield: 8 servings

Serving size: 1 kabob with ¼ cup salad

Nutrient analysis per serving: 143 calories, 19 gm protein, 8 gm carbohydrate, 4 gm fat, 1 gm fiber

*Good source of fiber

Mango Chicken Salad

½ cup salad greens
2 tsp chopped green onion
1 Tbsp lime juice
2 tsp rice vinegar
½ tsp cilantro
1 Tbsp olive oil
⅓ cup mango, peeled, sliced and cubed
1 avocado slice, cubed
4 tsp soy nuts
½ cup cooked skinless chicken, cubed

In a large bowl, combine salad greens and green onion. In a small
bowl, whisk together lime juice, vinegar, and cilantro. Gradually
whisk in oil until emulsified. Pour over salad vegetables and
toss. Sprinkle salad with mango, avocado, nuts, and chicken.
Serve immediately.

Yield: ~5 servings

Serving size: ½ cup salad

Nutrient analysis per serving: 141 calories, 7.5 gm protein, 8 gm
carbohydrate, 10 gm fat, 2.25 gm fiber

*Great source of fiber and healthy fat

Taco Salad

Festive tip:

Other salad topping ideas—crumbled tofu, corn, black beans, chopped jalapenos, green olives, red onion, or 1 avocado slice.

1 lb extra lean ground beef
½ cup chopped onion
1 garlic clove, minced
1 (1 oz) package taco seasoning
3 cups shredded lettuce
1 med tomato, chopped
½ cup reduced-fat shredded cheddar cheese
1 (4 oz) can sliced ripe olives, drained
Lettuce leaves
Tomato wedges

Dressing

¾ cup fat-free sour cream
1 Tbsp chopped green onion
1 Tbsp tomato sauce
¼ tsp cumin
¼ tsp chili powder
¼ tsp garlic salt

In a large skillet, cook ground beef with onion and garlic until meat is no longer pink. Add taco seasoning and mix well. Let stand 5 minutes. Add lettuce, tomato, cheese, and olives to skillet.

In a small bowl, combine dressing ingredients; mix well and pour over salad. Toss to coat.

Line bowls with lettuce leaves and fill with taco salad. Top with tomato wedges.

Yield: 8 servings

Serving size: 2 oz beef, ½ cup salad, and 1-2 Tbsp dressing

Nutrient analysis per serving: 210 calories, 18 gm protein, 8 gm carbohydrate, 12 gm fat, 1 gm fiber

*Good source fiber and healthy fat

Citrus Shrimp Salad

Festive tip:

Drizzle some of dressing on the outer edge of a colored plate. Sprinkle pecans on top of dressing. Serve salad in the middle of the plate.

2 Tbsp fat-free Italian salad dressing
1 Tbsp low-fat sour cream
2 tsp lemon juice
1 tsp Dijon mustard
1 tsp sugar-free orange marmalade
½ tsp lemon pepper
½ lb cooked med shrimp, peeled and deveined
2 cups romaine lettuce
1 cup fresh spinach leaves
1 Tbsp chopped green pepper
1 Tbsp chopped green onion
5 grapefruit slices
5 orange slices
¼ cup chopped pecans

In a large bowl, combine Italian dressing, sour cream, lemon juice, mustard, sugar-free orange marmalade, and lemon pepper and mix well. Add shrimp and toss to coat. In another large bowl, combine romaine lettuce and spinach leaves. Sprinkle with green pepper and green onion. Top with grapefruit and orange slices. Remove shrimp from dressing and place on top of salad. Drizzle salad with dressing and sprinkle with pecans.

Yield: 6 servings

Serving size: ~3 shrimp with ½ cup salad

Nutrient analysis per serving: 96 calories, 9 gm protein, 7 gm carbohydrate, 4 gm fat, 2.25 gm fiber

*Great source of fiber and healthy fat

Salmon Salad

Festive tip:

Take ½ of a whole wheat English muffin and top with salmon salad, tomato slice, onion slice and mozzarella cheese slice made with part skim milk. Place in toaster oven until English muffin is toasted and cheese is melted.

¼ cup chopped cucumber
2 Tbsp chopped celery
1 Tbsp chopped green onion
1 Tbsp slivered almonds
2 tsp diced pimento
2 tsp minced fresh parsley
¼ tsp dill
¼ tsp ground mustard
1 (6 oz) can boneless salmon, drained
¼ cup low-fat mayonnaise
2 Tbsp prepared horseradish
2 tsp lemon juice
⅛ tsp salt
⅛ tsp garlic salt
⅛ tsp lemon pepper

In a large bowl, combine the 1st 8 ingredients and mix well. Add salmon and toss gently. In a small bowl, combine mayonnaise, horseradish, lemon juice, salt, garlic salt, and lemon pepper and mix well. Fold mayonnaise mixture into salmon mixture. Cover and refrigerate 1-2 hours.

Yield: 4 servings

Serving size: 2 oz salad

Nutrient analysis per serving: 114 calories, 8 gm protein, 3.5 gm carbohydrate, 7.5 gm fat, .75 gm fiber

*Good source of healthy fat

Edamome Bean Salad

Festive tip:

Serve edamome salad with shrimp cocktail. OR use edamome in other salads or salad topper, in soups, as a substitute for lima beans, or as a salted small meal (like peanuts).

½ lb edamome beans (soybeans in the pod), frozen
1 tsp olive oil
½ tsp salt
2½ cups salad greens
1 small carrot, julienned
2 Tbsp chopped green onion
2 Tbsp diced fresh mushroom
1 Tbsp slivered almonds
1 Tbsp rice vinegar
1 Tbsp soy sauce
2 tsp lime juice
½ tsp ground ginger
⅛ tsp garlic powder
2 tsp sesame oil

In a medium saucepan, bring water to boil and boil edamome beans for 3 minutes. Pop beans out of pods. In a large bowl, combine olive oil and salt; add beans and toss to coat.

In a medium bowl, combine salad greens, carrot, green onion, mushroom, almonds, and beans.

In a small bowl, whisk together vinegar, soy sauce, lime juice, ground ginger, and garlic powder. Gradually whisk in sesame oil until emulsified. Toss with salad.

Yield: 4 servings

Serving size: ½ cup salad

Nutrient analysis per serving: 135 calories, 8 gm protein, 11 gm carbohydrate, 7 gm fat, 4 gm fiber

*Excellent source of fiber and healthy fat

Mardi Gras Bean Salad

1 (15 oz) can kidney beans, rinsed and drained
1 (15 oz) can black beans, rinsed and drained
1 small **green** pepper, chopped
1 small **tomato**, chopped
¼-½ cup chopped red onion
½ cup frozen corn, thawed
2 Tbsp rice vinegar
1 garlic clove, minced
½ tsp Worcestershire sauce
½ tsp hot pepper sauce
½ tsp seasoned salt
½ tsp pepper
¼ tsp Creole seasoning
2 Tbsp olive oil

In a large bowl, combine the 1st 6 ingredients and mix well. In a small bowl, whisk together vinegar, garlic, Worcestershire sauce, hot pepper sauce, seasoned salt, pepper, and Creole seasoning. Gradually whisk in oil until emulsified. Pour over bean salad and mix well. Chill thoroughly.

Yield: ~10 servings

Serving size: ½ cup salad

Nutrient analysis per serving: 109 calories, 5 gm protein, 15 gm carbohydrate, 3 gm fat, 6 gm fiber

*Excellent source of fiber

Insalata Caprese Salad

Festive tip:

To serve as appetizers—thread basil leaf, mozzarella cheese cube, and tomato wedge on a toothpick and have olive oil in a small bowl for dipping.

3 large tomatoes, cut into ¼" thick slices
1 lb fresh mozzarella cheese made with part skim milk, cut into ¼" thick slices
15-20 basil leaves
2 Tbsp olive oil
1 Tbsp pine nuts
Salt and pepper to taste

On a large plate, alternate layers of tomato, cheese, and basil leaves. Drizzle with olive oil. Sprinkle with pine nuts, salt, and pepper.

Yield: 16 servings

Serving size: 1 oz cheese slice, 1 tomato slice, 4 basil leaves, ~¼-½ tsp oil, and ⅛-¼ tsp nuts

Nutrient analysis per serving: 93 calories, 7 gm protein, 2 gm carbohydrate, 7 gm fat, .5 gm fiber

*Good source of healthy fat

Cottage Cheese Spinach Salad

Festive tip:

Place a few cottage cheese curds and pine nuts on red serving plates. Top with salad.

3 cups fresh spinach leaves
2 Tbsp pine nuts
1 Tbsp red wine vinegar
1½ tsp ground mustard
⅛ tsp garlic salt
1 tsp canola oil
½ cup fat-free cottage cheese

Place spinach leaves in a large bowl. Sprinkle with nuts. In a small bowl, whisk together vinegar, mustard, and garlic salt. Gradually whisk in oil until emulsified. Drizzle over spinach. Top with cottage cheese.

Yield: 2 servings

Serving size: ½ of salad

Nutrient Analysis per serving: 135 calories, 10 gm protein, 4 gm carbohydrate, 8.5 gm fat, 4.5 gm fiber

*Excellent source of fiber and healthy fat

Greek Salad

Festive tip:

Slice a tomato and place slices around edges of a black plate. Serve salad in the middle of the plate. Sprinkle with green onion slices.

1 (15 oz) can chickpeas or garbanzo beans, rinsed and drained
2 med tomatoes, chopped
1 (4 oz) can sliced ripe olives, drained
½ cup low-fat cottage cheese
2 Tbsp chopped onion
½ tsp garlic salt
½ tsp coarse ground black pepper
1 Tbsp olive oil
1 Tbsp lemon juice

In a large bowl, combine the 1st 7 ingredients and mix well. In a small bowl, whisk together oil and lemon juice until emulsified. Add to salad and mix well.

Yield: ~8 servings

Serving size: ½ cup salad

Nutrient analysis per serving: 112 calories, 4.5 gm protein, 15 gm carbohydrate, 4 gm fat, 3.25 gm fiber

*Excellent source of fiber and healthy fat

Strawberry Spinach Salad

Festive tip:

Thread strawberry, cream cheese cubes, and lime wedges on skewers. Serve salad on white plates and place skewers beside salad.

3 cups torn spinach leaves
5 large strawberries
½ cup slivered almonds
¼ cup sunflower seed kernels
2 oz light cream cheese, cubed

Sweet Lime Vinaigrette

2 Tbsp lime juice
1 Tbsp minced green onion
1 tsp Splenda®
⅛ tsp celery seed
⅛ tsp paprika
⅛ tsp salt
2 Tbsp canola oil

In a large bowl, combine spinach leaves, strawberries, almonds, and sunflower seeds. In a small bowl, whisk together lime juice, green onion, Splenda®, celery seed, paprika, and salt. Gradually whisk in oil until emulsified. Pour over salad and toss to coat. Sprinkle with cream cheese. Serve immediately.

Yield: 6 servings

Serving size: ~½ cup salad

Nutrient analysis per serving: 184 calories, 5 gm protein, 10 gm carbohydrate, 15 gm fat, 5 gm fiber

*Excellent source of fiber and healthy fat

Fruit Salad

Festive tip:

Serve fruit salad in
stemmed glasses.
Sprinkle with nuts
and garnish rim
of glasses with
mandarin oranges.

½ cup light cream cheese, softened
1 Tbsp natural flavored protein powder
1 Tbsp Splenda®
1 (4 oz) can mandarin oranges in its own juice, drained
1 (4 oz) can crushed pineapple in its own juice, drained
½ tsp coconut extract
½ cup sugar-free whipped topping
1 Tbsp chopped pecans

In a large bowl, beat cream cheese, protein powder, and Splenda®
until smooth. Add oranges, pineapples, and coconut extract and
mix well. Fold in whipped topping. Top with nuts. Cover and
refrigerate 2-4 hours.

Yield: 4 servings

Serving size: ~½ cup salad

Nutrient analysis per serving: 125 calories, 6 gm protein, 10 gm
carbohydrate, 7 gm fat, .75 gm fiber

Festive tip:

Add this dressing to ground turkey for a livelier turkey burger.

Thousand Island Salad Dressing

1 cup low-fat mayonnaise
¼ cup tomato sauce
1 boiled egg, finely chopped
2 Tbsp rice vinegar
1 small celery stalk, finely chopped
2 Tbsp finely chopped onion
1½ Tbsp Splenda®
1 Tbsp finely chopped pimento

In a condiment bottle, combine all ingredients and mix well. Chill thoroughly.

Yield: ~13 servings

Serving size: 2 Tbsp dressing

Nutrient analysis per serving: 55 calories, 1 gm protein, 4 gm carbohydrate, 4 gm fat, 0 gm fiber

French Salad Dressing

Festive tip:

Use this dressing as a marinade for flank steak to make it tender and tasty.

¼ cup low-fat mayonnaise
¼ cup tomato sauce
2 Tbsp rice vinegar
¼ cup Splenda®
¼ tsp ground mustard
¼ tsp garlic salt
⅛ tsp white pepper
⅛ tsp paprika
¼ cup canola oil

In a condiment bottle, combine the 1ˢᵗ 8 ingredients and mix well. Gradually add oil until emulsified. Chill thoroughly.

Yield: ~9 servings

Serving size: 2 Tbsp dressing

Nutrient analysis per serving: 81 calories, 0 gm protein, 2 gm carbohydrate, 8 gm fat, 0 gm fiber

*Great source of healthy fat

Raspberry-Sesame Vinaigrette

Festive tip:

Use this vinaigrette over salad greens topped with chicken, walnuts, and a few bing cherries, pitted.

1 Tbsp Splenda®
½ tsp ground mustard
¼ tsp garlic salt
¼ tsp paprika
⅓ cup sugar-free seedless raspberry preserves
¼ cup lemon juice
1 Tbsp rice vinegar
⅓ cup canola oil
2 Tbsp sesame oil
1 Tbsp toasted sesame seeds

In a medium bowl, combine the 1ˢᵗ 4 ingredients. Whisk in sugar-free preserves, lemon juice, and vinegar until well mixed. Gradually whisk in oils until emulsified. Add sesame seeds and mix well. Chill thoroughly.

Yield: 9 servings

Serving size: 2 Tbsp vinaigrette

Nutrient analysis per serving: 89 calories, 0 gm protein, 4 gm carbohydrate, 9 gm fat, 0 gm fiber

*Great source of healthy fat

Lemon-Caper Vinaigrette

Festive tip:

Serve this vinaigrette over salad topped with smoked salmon, seared tuna, or grilled halibut. Also drizzle over steamed asparagus or broccoli.

2 Tbsp lemon juice
2 Tbsp capers
2 tsp lemon zest
2 tsp Dijon mustard
1 tsp parsley
½ tsp pepper
¼ tsp garlic salt
¼ tsp salt
6 Tbsp olive oil

In a medium bowl, whisk together the 1st 8 ingredients. Gradually whisk in oil until emulsified. Chill thoroughly.

Yield: 12 servings

Serving size: 1 Tbsp vinaigrette

Nutrient analysis per serving: 62 calories, 0 gm protein, 0 gm carbohydrate, 6 gm fat, 0 gm fiber

*Great source of healthy fat

Poppy Seed Vinaigrette

Festive tip:

Serve this vinaigrette over spinach salad topped with mandarin oranges, sliced mushrooms, red onions, and chopped egg whites.

1 cup Splenda®
6 Tbsp white vinegar
2 Tbsp lime juice
1 tsp poppy seeds
½ tsp salt
¼ tsp ground mustard
⅛ tsp garlic powder
¼ cup canola oil

In a medium bowl, whisk together the 1st 7 ingredients. Gradually whisk in oil until emulsified. Chill thoroughly.

Yield: ~14 servings

Serving size: 2 Tbsp vinaigrette

Nutrient analysis per serving: 43 calories, 0 gm protein, 2 gm carbohydrate, 4 gm fat, 0 gm fiber

*Great source of healthy fat

Horseradish Sauce

Festive tip:

Add 1 Tbsp of horseradish sauce to crab salad, scrambled eggs, or turkey sausage.

½ cup low-fat mayonnaise
½ cup nonfat plain yogurt
2 Tbsp prepared horseradish
2 tsp lemon juice
½ tsp garlic salt
½ tsp ground mustard
Skim milk

In a condiment bottle, combine mayonnaise, yogurt, horseradish, lemon juice, garlic salt, and ground mustard and mix well. Use skim milk to thin to desired consistency. Serve with vegetables or over fish, beef, and other meats.

Yield: 9 servings

Serving size: 2 Tbsp sauce

Nutrient analysis per serving: 43 calories, 1 gm protein, 4 gm carbohydrate, 3 gm fat, 0 gm fiber

Mango Pineapple Salsa

Festive tip:

Serve salsa in a
square-shaped bowl.
Spoon over grilled
meat.

½ cup mango, peeled and chopped
¼ cup frozen pineapple chunks, thawed and chopped
2 tsp chopped fresh parsley
2 tsp chopped onion
1 tsp diced jalapeno pepper
1 tsp lime juice

In a small bowl, combine all ingredients and mix well. Cover
and refrigerate for 1 hour. Serve over chicken, fish, or other
lean meats.

Yield: 4-5 servings

Serving size: 2 Tbsp salsa

Nutrient analysis per serving: 18 calories, 0 gm protein, 4.5 gm
carbohydrate, 0 gm fat, .5 gm fiber

Avocado Salsa

Festive tip:

Make huevos rancheros—place a warm corn tortilla on a plate; top with black beans, then egg and top with avocado salsa.

1 small tomato, chopped
½ cup frozen corn, thawed
1 (4 oz) can chopped ripe olives, drained
1 Tbsp chopped onion
3 Tbsp lime juice
2 Tbsp cider vinegar
1 Tbsp olive oil
1 tsp cilantro
1 tsp garlic salt
½ tsp pepper
⅛ tsp cayenne pepper
2 ripe avocados, peeled, pitted, and diced

In a large bowl, combine the 1st 4 ingredients. In a small bowl, combine lime juice, vinegar, oil, cilantro, garlic salt, pepper, and cayenne pepper and mix well. Add lime juice mixture to tomato mixture and toss to coat. Gently stir in avocados before serving to maintain chunky consistency. Serve with vegetables or over fish, chicken, or other lean meats.

Yield: 15 servings

Serving size: ¼ cup salsa

Nutrient analysis per serving: 63 calories, 1 gm protein, 4 gm carbohydrate, 5 gm fat, 2 gm fiber

*Great source of fiber and healthy fat

Berry Salsa

Festive tip:

Serve salsa in a white bowl to bring out the "berry" beautiful colors. Spoon over grilled meats.

½ cup chopped strawberries
¼ cup chopped raspberries
2 Tbsp Splenda®
2 tsp diced jalapeno pepper
1 tsp lemon juice
2 tsp slivered almonds

In a small bowl, combine the 1st 5 ingredients and mix well. Cover and refrigerate ~1 hour. Just before serving, add almonds and stir. Serve over chicken, fish, or other lean meats.

Yield: 4-5 servings

Serving size: 2 Tbsp salsa

Nutrient analysis per serving: 20 calories, .5 gm protein, 3 gm carbohydrate, .75 gm fat, 1 gm fiber

*Good source of fiber

Black Bean Salsa

1 (15 oz) can black beans, rinsed and drained
½ cup chopped tomato
¼ cup chopped onion
1 jalapeno pepper, diced
2 tsp chopped fresh cilantro
1 tsp lime juice
½ tsp garlic salt
½ tsp cracked pepper

In a medium bowl, combine all ingredients and mix well. Cover and refrigerate for 1-2 hours. Serve with vegetables or over fish, chicken, or other lean meats.

Yield: 21 servings

Serving size: 2 Tbsp salsa

Nutrient analysis per serving: 22 calories, 1.25 gm protein, 3.5 gm carbohydrate, 0 gm fat, 1.25 gm fiber

*Good source of fiber

Chile-Citrus Salsa

Festive tip:

Mix some of salsa juice with olive oil for a zesty vinaigrette or mix with other low-fat salad dressings for added zing.

1 serrano chili pepper, seeded and chopped
1 small orange, peeled, sectioned, and cut into bite size pieces
1 lemon, peeled, sectioned, and cut into bite size pieces
1 key lime, peeled, sectioned, and cut into bite size pieces
2 Tbsp chopped onion
2-3 mint leaves, chopped
1 Tbsp Splenda®
1 Tbsp lime juice
¼ tsp salt

In a medium bowl, combine the 1ˢᵗ 6 ingredients. In a small bowl, combine Splenda®, lime juice, and salt; mix well and drizzle over salsa. Mix gently. Cover and chill ~2 hours. Serve over chicken, fish, or other lean meats.

Yield: ~11 servings

Serving size: 2 Tbsp salsa

Nutrient analysis per serving: 11 calories, .25 gm protein, 3 gm carbohydrate, 0 gm fat, 1 gm fiber

*Good source of fiber

Sweet Bites

Vanilla Custard
Apple Soufflé
High Protein Brownies
Crustless Cheesecake
Cherry Cheesecake Dessert
Creamy Chocolate Dessert
Fruit Soup
Stuffed Strawberries
Pumpkin Dip
Tropical Fruit Dip
Chocolate Fruit Dip
Creamy Peanut Butter Dip
Peanut Butter and Chocolate Parfait
Blueberry Lemon Parfaits
3-Layer Gelatin Salad
Creamy Strawberry Dessert
Dreamsicle Dessert
Banana Pudding
Tropical Fruit Smoothie
Frozen Fruit Cups
Strawberry Frozen Yogurt
Frozen Yogurt Pops
Vanilla Mocha Ice
Vanilla Ice Cream with Peanut Butter Sundae Sauce

For the last nineteen years I've taught at a Bible camp in the NM mountains. The elevation and my asthma, coupled with my aching knees, frequently left me "staging" my movement from one part of the camp to another. I would plan rest stops along the way and plan ahead to ensure that I didn't have to make multiple trips. A year after RNY, and the loss of 210 pounds, I can run between activity areas and I don't have asthma any more.

I sought freedom from food "being the boss of me." RNY provides immediate negative consequences if I deviate from appropriate eating, and I need that continuity in my life. My commitment to this process includes eating, drinking and exercising in a way that promotes a healthy lifestyle.

I would not trade one year of my being overweight for the lessons I've learned. I am barely scratching the surface of what I can learn from spending most of my life as obese, then morbidly obese, and finally super obese. I am 48 years old and I have much of a lifetime to learn and then proclaim these lessons; I am excited and happy about the moments ahead.

Vanilla Custard

1 egg
½ cup skim milk
¼ cup Splenda®
1 tsp vanilla extract
⅛ tsp salt
¼ tsp cinnamon

In a medium bowl, beat the 1st 5 ingredients together until well mixed and pour into 2 (6 oz) custard cups coated with nonstick cooking spray. Sprinkle with cinnamon.

Place custard cups in a 1 Qt baking dish filled with 1" hot water. Bake @ 325° for 40-45 minutes or until knife inserted in center comes out clean. Remove and place in cool water. Chill thoroughly, ~2 hours.

Yield: 2 servings

Serving size: 1 custard

Nutrient analysis per serving: 78 calories, 6 gm protein, 7 gm carbohydrate, 3 gm fat, 0 gm fiber

Apple Soufflé

Festive tip:

Sprinkle a plate with slivered almonds. Place warm apple soufflé on top, add a dollop of sugar-free whipped topping and sprinkle with cinnamon OR serve cold with fruit soup.

3 med baking apples, peeled, cored, and cut into 1" pieces
½ cup water
1 cup ricotta cheese made with part skim milk
1 (6 oz) container of low-fat, sugar-free vanilla yogurt
¾ cup Splenda®
2 Tbsp cream of wheat, dry
Pinch of salt
4 egg whites

In a medium saucepan, combine apples and water. Bring to a rolling boil. Cover, reduce heat, and simmer, stirring frequently for 10 minutes or until apples are tender. Drain water. Add ricotta cheese, yogurt, Splenda®, cream of wheat, and salt. Stir until well blended. Set aside. In a large bowl, beat egg whites until stiff peaks form. Fold egg whites into cooled apple mixture. Pour into a 2 Qt baking dish coated with nonstick cooking spray. Bake @ 350° for 45-50 minutes or until soufflé is puffed and browned.

Yield: 12 servings

Serving size: 1/12th soufflé

Nutrient Analysis per serving: 65 calories, 5 gm protein, 9 gm carbohydrate, 1.5 gm fat, .25 gm fiber

High Protein Brownies

Festive tip:

Serve brownies on
a white plate and
top brownies with
fresh raspberries and
chopped pistachios.
Garnish edge of
plate with fresh
raspberries.

¼ cup baking cocoa
¼ cup boiling water
4 eggs
1¼ cups Splenda®
¼ cup natural flavored protein powder
½ cup whole wheat flour
½ tsp baking soda
¼ tsp salt
¼ cup unsweetened applesauce
2 Tbsp canola oil
1½ tsp vanilla extract

In a small bowl, dissolve cocoa in water. Set aside to cool. In
a medium bowl, beat eggs until lightened ~1-2 minutes. Add
Splenda® and beat until smooth. Drizzle chocolate mixture into
egg mixture while beating until mixture is well blended. In a
small bowl, combine protein powder, whole wheat flour, baking
soda, and salt and mix well. Add protein powder mixture to
chocolate mixture and beat until well blended. Add applesauce,
oil, and vanilla extract and beat another 30 seconds. Pour batter
into an 8 x 8 baking dish coated with non-stick cooking spray.
Bake @ 350° for 20-25 minutes or until toothpick inserted in
center comes out clean. Let cool completely before cutting.

Yield: 9 servings

Serving size: 1 brownie

Nutrient analysis per serving: 117 calories, 7 gm protein, 10.5
gm carbohydrate, 5.5 gm fat, 1.5 gm fiber

*Good source of fiber and healthy fat

Crustless Cheesecake

Festive tip:

Garnish top of
cheesecake with
lemon zest curls
around raspberries.

1 (.3oz) package sugar-free lemon gelatin mix
⅓ cup boiling water
1 (8 oz) package light cream cheese
1 cup low-fat cottage cheese
2 cups sugar-free whipped topping
Fresh raspberries

In a small bowl, dissolve gelatin mix in water. In a large bowl, blend cream cheese and cottage cheese until smooth. Add gelatin mixture to cream cheese mixture and stir well. Fold in whipped topping. Pour into a 9" pie plate. Refrigerate ~4 hours or overnight. Top with fresh raspberries.

Yield: 10 servings

Serving size: 1/10th cheesecake

Nutrient Analysis per serving: 135 calories, 6 gm protein, 12 gm carbohydrate, 7 gm fat, .25 gm fiber

Cherry Cheesecake Dessert

Festive tip:

Serve dessert in champagne flutes instead of bowls. Sprinkle with nut topping.

1 (8 oz) package light cream cheese, softened
¾ cup Splenda®
½ cup low-fat sour cream
½ cup sugar-free whipped topping
½ tsp vanilla extract
1½ cups no added sugar cherry pie filling

In a large bowl, beat cream cheese, Splenda®, sour cream, whipped topping, and vanilla extract until smooth.

In 6 small bowls, divide cream cheese mixture for bottom layers. Top each with ¼ cup cherry pie filling. Chill for at least 2 hours.

Yield: 6 servings

Serving size: 1 dessert

Nutrient analysis per serving: 168 calories, 5 gm protein, 15 gm carbohydrate, 10 gm fat, 0 gm fiber

Creamy Chocolate Dessert

Festive tip:

Serve dessert in the center of a white plate topped with fresh raspberries and a dollop of sugar-free whipped topping. Spoon small amounts (dime size) of sugar-free raspberry preserves around the edge of the plate.

1 egg white
½ cup whole wheat flour
¼ cup finely chopped walnuts
2 Tbsp canola oil
4 oz light cream cheese
¼ cup low-fat sour cream
⅓ cup Splenda®
1 (1.4 oz) package sugar-free chocolate instant pudding mix
2 cups skim milk

For Crust: In a medium bowl, combine egg white, flour, walnuts, and oil until moistened. Press into bottom and sides of a 1½ Qt baking dish coated with nonstick cooking spray. Bake @ 350° for 15-20 minutes. Cool to room temp.

For Cream Cheese Layer: In a medium bowl, beat cream cheese, sour cream, and Splenda® until smooth. Pour over crust layer.

For Chocolate Layer: In a medium bowl, beat chocolate pudding mix and milk for 2 minutes. Spread over cream cheese layer. Chill for ~1 hour.

Yield: 9 servings

Serving size: 1/9th dessert

Nutrient analysis per serving: 129 calories, 5 gm protein, 11 gm carbohydrate, 7.5 gm fat, 1 gm fiber

*Good source of fiber and healthy fat

Fruit Soup

1 pint fresh raspberries
2 cups water
1½ cups Splenda®
1 cup nonfat plain yogurt
2 Tbsp lemon juice
1 Tbsp natural flavored protein powder
1 Tbsp lemon zest
¼ tsp ground ginger
¼ tsp coriander
¼ tsp cinnamon

In a food processor, puree all ingredients until very smooth. Chill thoroughly.

Yield: 9 servings

Serving size: ½ cup soup

Nutrient analysis per serving: 51 calories, 3 gm protein, 10 gm carbohydrate, 0 gm fat, 2 gm fiber

*Great source of fiber

Stuffed Strawberries

12 large strawberries
½ cup light cream cheese
2 Tbsp Splenda®
1 Tbsp natural flavored protein powder
1 tsp sugar-free strawberry preserves

Remove stems from strawberries and place stem side down on a plate. Cut a deep "X" into the top of each strawberry and spread apart carefully. In a small bowl, beat cream cheese, Splenda®, protein powder, and sugar-free preserves until smooth. Pipe or spoon cream cheese mixture into the middle of berries. Chill in refrigerator until ready to serve.

Yield: ~6 servings

Serving size: 2 stuffed strawberries

Nutrient analysis per serving: 64 calories, 4 gm protein, 4 gm carbohydrate, 4 gm fat, 1.25 gm fiber

*Good source of fiber

Pumpkin Dip

Festive tip:

Cut top off of miniature pumpkin and remove seeds. Clean inside of pumpkin well. Serve pumpkin dip in pumpkin bowl on a black plate with apple and pear slices around it. Dip fruit slices in lemon juice to prevent browning.

1 (8 oz) package light cream cheese, softened
1 (15 oz) can pumpkin
2 cups Splenda®
2 Tbsp natural flavored protein powder
1 tsp cinnamon
½ tsp ground ginger
½ tsp vanilla extract
½ tsp maple extract
¼ tsp ground cloves
Apple and pear slices

In a large bowl, beat cream cheese, pumpkin, Splenda®, and protein powder until smooth. Add cinnamon, ginger, vanilla and maple extracts, and cloves and mix well. Chill thoroughly and serve with apple and pear slices.

Yield: 12 servings

Serving size: ¼ cup dip with 3 apple or pear slices

Nutrient Analysis per serving: 94 calories, 4.25 gm protein, 12.75 gm carbohydrate, 3.5 gm fat, .75 gm fiber

Tropical Fruit Dip

Festive tip:

Take 2 orange slices, 2 blueberries, 2 strawberries, and 2 peach slices and arrange them on top of dip to make a smiley face. Place orange slices as eyes and blueberries on top of orange slices for eyeballs. Place 3 strawberry halves for cheeks and nose. Place peach slices for the mouth.

1½ cups skim milk
1 cup low-fat sour cream
1 (1.4 oz) package sugar-free banana pudding mix
1 Tbsp Splenda®
¼ tsp coconut extract
¼ tsp orange zest
Fresh fruit

In a medium bowl, combine milk, sour cream, pudding mix, Splenda®, coconut extract, and orange zest and mix well. Cover and refrigerate for ~1 hour. Serve with fruit.

Yield: 5 servings

Serving size: ½ cup dip with ¼ cup fruit

Nutrient analysis per serving: 110 calories, 4.25 gm protein, 10.75 gm carbohydrate, 6 gm fat, .75 gm fiber

Chocolate Fruit Dip

Festive tip:

Serve chocolate dip
in heart-shaped dish
on top of a plate.
Serve strawberries in
wine glasses.

1 (1.4 oz) package sugar-free instant chocolate pudding mix
2 cups skim milk
¼ cup natural flavored protein powder
¼ cup low-fat sour cream
2 Tbsp Splenda®
½ tsp orange zest
Fresh strawberries

In a medium bowl, beat chocolate pudding mix with milk and
protein powder for 2 minutes. Add sour cream, Splenda®, and
orange zest and beat until well mixed. Cover and refrigerate at
least 10 minutes. Serve with strawberries.

Yield: 11 servings

Serving size: ¼ cup dip with ¼ cup strawberries

Nutrient analysis per serving: 63 calories, 5.25 gm protein, 8.75
gm carbohydrate, 0 gm fat, .75 gm fiber

Creamy Peanut Butter Dip

1 (4 oz) container low-carbohydrate vanilla yogurt
3 Tbsp milk
½ cup natural peanut butter
2 tsp Splenda®
¼ tsp maple extract
⅛ tsp cinnamon
Apple and pear slices or celery sticks

In a medium bowl, combine yogurt, milk, peanut butter, Splenda®, maple extract, and cinnamon and mix well. Chill thoroughly and serve with apple or pear slices or celery sticks.

*This recipe used Dannon® Light and Fit sugar/carb control yogurt.

Yield: 5 servings

Serving size: ¼ cup dip with 3 apple or pear slices

Nutrient analysis per serving: 197 calories, 7.75 gm protein, 9.75 gm carbohydrate, 13 gm fat, 2.25 gm fiber

*Great source of fiber and healthy fat

Peanut Butter and Chocolate Parfait

1 (1.4 oz) package sugar-free instant chocolate pudding mix
2 cups skim milk
1½ cups sugar-free whipped topping + 2 Tbsp, divided
½ cup natural peanut butter
¼ tsp cinnamon

In a medium bowl, beat pudding mix with milk for 2 minutes.
Refrigerate.

In another medium bowl, combine 1½ cups whipped topping,
peanut butter, and cinnamon and mix well. In 2 parfait glasses,
alternate layers of chocolate pudding and peanut butter mixture.
Chill thoroughly. Top each parfait with 1 Tbsp whipped topping.

Yield: ~8 servings

Serving size: ½ cup parfait

Nutrient analysis per serving: 176 calories, 7 gm protein, 15 gm
carbohydrate, 10 gm fat, 1 gm fiber

*Good source of fiber and healthy fat

Blueberry Lemon Parfaits

Festive tip:

Top parfaits with a few blueberries and mint sprig. Garnish rim of glasses with lemon wedges.

1½ cups fresh blueberries
2 Tbsp Splenda®
1 (.3 oz) package sugar-free lemon gelatin mix
1 Tbsp natural flavored protein powder
½ cup boiling water
2 (8 oz) containers nonfat plain yogurt

In a medium bowl, combine blueberries and Splenda® and mix well. In a large bowl, dissolve gelatin mix and protein powder in water. Stir yogurt into gelatin mixture until smooth.
In 2 parfait glasses, divide ½ of yogurt mixture evenly for bottom layers. Spoon blueberries evenly over the yogurt layers. Top blueberry layers with remaining ½ of yogurt mixture. Chill for ~1 hour.

Yield: ~8 servings

Serving size: ½ cup parfait

Nutrient analysis per serving: 55 calories, 3 gm protein, 10 gm carbohydrate, 0 gm fat, 1 gm fiber

*Good source of fiber

3-Layer Gelatin Salad

Festive tip:

Use decorative gelatin mold to prepare gelatin. Turn gelatin onto a clear platter and garnish with cherries and mint leaves.

Layer 1:
1 (.3 oz) package sugar-free lime gelatin mix
1 Tbsp natural flavored protein powder
¾ cup boiling water
¾ cup cold water
1 (8 oz) can crushed pineapple in its own juice, drained

Layer 2:
1 (.3 oz) package sugar-free orange gelatin mix
1 cup boiling water
4 oz light cream cheese, softened
½ cup low-fat sour cream
2 Tbsp Splenda®

Layer 3:
1 (.3 oz) package sugar-free cherry gelatin mix
¾ cup boiling water
¾ cup cold water
1½ cups sugar-free whipped topping, divided

Layer 1: In a 2 Qt bowl, dissolve lime gelatin mix and protein powder in boiling water; add cold water. Stir in pineapple. Refrigerate, stirring occasionally until ALMOST set, then let alone until firm.

Layer 2: In a medium bowl, dissolve orange gelatin mix in boiling water. In another medium bowl, beat cream cheese, sour cream, and Splenda® until smooth. Fold cream cheese mixture into orange gelatin. Spoon over lime gelatin layer. Refrigerate until firm.

Layer 3: In a medium bowl, dissolve cherry gelatin mix in boiling water; add cold water. Refrigerate until ALMOST set; fold in ½ cup whipped topping and spoon over orange gelatin layer. Refrigerate 4-6 hours or overnight. Top with remaining whipped topping.

Yield: 14 servings

Serving size: ½ cup gelatin salad

Nutrient analysis per serving: 62 calories, 3 gm protein, 5 gm carbohydrate, 3 gm fat, .25 gm fiber

Creamy Strawberry Dessert

1 (.3 oz) package sugar-free strawberry gelatin mix
1 cup boiling water
1 cup cold water
1 (4 oz) container low carbohydrate strawberry yogurt
½ cup sliced fresh strawberries
¼ cup low-fat sour cream
2 Tbsp Splenda®

In a large bowl, dissolve gelatin mix in boiling water. Add cold
water and yogurt and mix well. Chill in refrigerator for ~1 hour.
Stir in strawberries, sour cream, and Splenda® until well mixed.
Chill thoroughly.

*This recipe used Dannon® Light and Fit sugar/carb control
yogurt.

Yield: ~6 servings

Serving size: ½ cup dessert

Nutrient analysis per serving: 33 calories, 2 gm protein, 2.5 gm
carbohydrate, 1 gm fat, .25 gm fiber

Dreamsicle Dessert

Festive tip:

Serve dessert in a
white bowl and place
mandarin oranges
around the edges of
the bowl. Spoon a
dollop of sugar-free
whipped topping
in the center of the
dessert and place
a few mint leaves
in the top of the
whipped topping.

1 (.3 oz) package sugar-free orange gelatin mix
1 cup boiling water
2 Tbsp Splenda®
1 Tbsp natural protein powder
¼ tsp vanilla extract
1 cup sugar-free whipped topping

In a medium bowl, dissolve gelatin mix in water. Add Splenda®,
protein powder, and vanilla extract and mix well. Cover and
refrigerate ~2 hours.

Beat gelatin on high speed for 2 minutes. Add whipped topping
and beat on low speed until smooth.

Yield: 2 servings

Serving size: ¾-1 cup dessert

Nutrient analysis per serving: 33 calories, 5 gm protein, 5 gm
carbohydrate, .25 gm fat, 0 gm fiber

Banana Pudding

Festive tip:

Serve pudding over strawberries in wine glasses. Top with a strawberry and garnish with 2 mint leaves.

1 (3.4 oz) package sugar-free instant vanilla pudding mix
2 cups skim milk
½ cup low-fat sour cream
¼ cup natural flavored protein powder
2 Tbsp Splenda®
1 small banana, sliced
½ cup chopped pecans

In a large bowl, combine pudding mix, milk, sour cream, protein powder, and Splenda® and beat on high for 1 minute. Fold in the banana slices. Cover and refrigerate ~1 hour or longer. Sprinkle with pecans before serving.

Yield: ~7 servings

Serving size: ½ cup pudding

Nutrient analysis per serving: 142 calories, 9 gm protein, 9 gm carbohydrate, 8 gm fat, 1 gm fiber

*Good source of fiber and healthy fat

Tropical Fruit Smoothie

Festive tip:

Spoon a small
amount of crushed
pineapple on top of
smoothie and place
slices of strawberry
next to pineapple.

½ cup evaporated skim milk
3 Tbsp Splenda®
1 (4 oz) container low carbohydrate vanilla yogurt
½ (8 oz) can crushed pineapple in its own juice, drained
3 strawberries, sliced
2 Tbsp lemon juice
¼ tsp coconut extract
½ cup crushed ice

In a blender, combine evaporated skim milk, Splenda®, yogurt,
pineapple, strawberries, lemon juice, and coconut extract and
pulse until smooth. Add ice and pulse until smooth, adding
more ice if necessary to make it desired thickness. Serve
immediately.

*This recipe used Dannon® Light and Fit sugar/carb control
yogurt.

Yield: 5 servings

Serving size: ~ ½ cup smoothie

Nutrient Analysis per serving: 59 calories, 3 gm protein, 10 gm
carbohydrate, 0 gm fat, .5 gm fiber

Frozen Fruit Cups

1 (.3 oz) package sugar-free lemon gelatin mix
1 cup boiling water
1 cup nonfat plain yogurt
3 Tbsp Splenda®
½ cup fresh strawberries, halved
1 (8 oz) can pineapple tidbits in its own juice, drained
1 firm banana, sliced
12 (3 oz) paper cups

In a medium bowl, dissolve gelatin mix in boiling water. Stir in yogurt, Splenda®, strawberries, pineapple, and banana and mix well. Place cups on a cookie sheet and spoon gelatin mixture into cups. Freeze until frozen through, ~3 hours. Let stand at room temp ~20 minutes before serving.

Yield: 12 servings

Serving size: 1 fruit cup

Nutrient analysis per serving: 35 calories, 1.5 gm protein, 7 gm carbohydrate, 0 gm fat, .5 gm fiber

Strawberry Frozen Yogurt

Festive tip:

Serve yogurt in a black bowl and top with strawberry and kiwi slices. Garnish with mint leaves.

1 cup nonfat plain yogurt
½ cup instant nonfat dry milk
½ cup low-fat sour cream
2 Tbsp Splenda®
¼ cup sugar-free strawberry preserves
1 envelope unflavored gelatin
1¼ cups cold water, divided
2 tsp vanilla extract

In a blender, combine yogurt, dry milk, sour cream, Splenda®, and sugar-free preserves and pulse until smooth. In a small saucepan, sprinkle gelatin over ¼ cup cold water. Let stand 1 minute and cook over medium heat until gelatin dissolves, stirring frequently. Add gelatin mixture, remaining water, and vanilla extract to yogurt mixture and pulse until smooth.

Pour mixture into an ice cream maker and freeze according to manufacturer's instructions.

Yield: ~7 servings

Serving size: ½ cup frozen yogurt

Nutrient analysis per serving: 93 calories, 6 gm protein, 14 gm carbohydrate, 2 gm fat, 0 gm fiber

Frozen Yogurt Pops

Festive tip:

Use fun and colorful
popsicle molds
instead of paper cups
and popsicle sticks.

1 cup skim milk
3 Tbsp Splenda®
½ cup fresh strawberries, halved
1 (4 oz) container low carbohydrate strawberry yogurt
10 of each-(3 oz) paper cups and popsicle sticks

In a blender, combine milk, Splenda®, strawberries, and yogurt
and pulse until smooth. Pour into cups and place on a cookie
sheet; freeze until frozen through, ~3 hours. When partially
frozen, place a popsicle stick in each cup. Let pops thaw slightly
to pull out of cups.

*This recipe used Dannon® Light and Fit sugar/carb control
yogurt.

Yield: 10 servings

Serving size: 1 yogurt pop

Nutrient analysis per serving: 21 calories, 2 gm protein, 3 gm
carbohydrate, .5 gm fat, .25 gm fiber

Fudge Pops

Festive tip:

Use colored popsicle sticks or draw faces on the tip of the popsicle stick that will be standing out of the fudge pop.

1 (1.4 oz) package sugar-free instant chocolate pudding mix
¼ cup Splenda®
1 Tbsp natural flavored protein powder
1½ cups skim milk
1 (12 oz) can evaporated skim milk
10-12 of each-(3 oz) paper cups and popsicle sticks

In a small bowl, combine pudding mix, Splenda®, and protein powder and mix well. In a large bowl, combine skim milk and evaporated skim milk. Sprinkle pudding mixture into milk mixture and stir with wire whisk until smooth.

Pour into cups and place on a cookie sheet. Freeze until frozen through, ~3 hours. When partially frozen, place a popsicle stick in each cup. Let pops thaw slightly to pull out of cups.

Yield: 10-12 servings

Serving size: 1 fudge pop

Nutrient analysis per serving: 51 calories, 5 gm protein, 8 gm carbohydrate, 0 gm fat, 0 gm fiber

Vanilla Mocha Ice

Festive tip:

Make variations
of mocha ice: add
almond extract,
cinnamon, or frozen
raspberries to mocha
ice before freezing.

2 cups sugar-free whipped topping
1½ cups brewed coffee
3 Tbsp sugar-free vanilla flavored coffee syrup (with no sugar
alcohols)
2 Tbsp natural flavored protein powder
1 Tbsp cocoa
10-12 of each-(3 oz) paper cups and popsicle sticks

In a blender, combine whipped topping, coffee, coffee syrup,
protein powder, and cocoa and pulse until smooth. Pour into
cups and place on a cookie sheet. Freeze until frozen through,
~3 hours. When partially frozen, place a popsicle stick in each
cup. Let mocha ice thaw slightly to pull out of cup.

*This recipe used DaVinci® Sugar-free Gourmet Coffee Syrup

Yield: 10-12 servings

Serving size: 1 mocha ice

Nutrient analysis per serving: 38 calories, 1.5 gm protein, 4.5
gm carbohydrate, 2 gm fat, 0 gm fiber

Vanilla Ice Cream w/ Peanut Butter Sauce

6 cups sugar-free whipped topping
1 (12 oz) can evaporated skim milk
4 egg yolks
1¾ cups Splenda®
2 tsp vanilla extract

Peanut Butter Sauce

¾ cup sugar-free apricot preserves
½ cup natural peanut butter

In a large saucepan, combine whipped topping and evaporated skim milk and cook over low heat. Whisk in egg yolks, one at a time and continue to cook over low heat, stirring constantly (until mixture coats the back of a spoon) ~8 minutes. Do not let boil. Remove from heat.

Whisk in Splenda® and vanilla extract. Place in freezer to cool. Pour into an ice cream maker and freeze according to manufacturer's instructions.

For sauce:
In a small saucepan, heat sugar-free preserves and peanut butter until melted, stirring frequently. Serve warm over ice cream.

Yield: ~25 servings

Serving Size: ~¼ cup ice cream with ~2 tsp of sundae sauce

Nutrient Analysis per serving: 103 calories, 3 gm protein, 12 gm carbohydrate, 5 gm fat, .5 gm fiber

References

1. Aills, Linda, R.D.; Blankenship, Jeanne, M.S., R.D.; Buffington, Ph.D; Furado, Margaret, M.S., R.D.; Parrott, Julie, M.S., R.D. Bariatric Nutrition: Suggestions for the Surgical Weight Loss Patient. Surgery for Obesity and Related Diseases 2008; 4(4S).
2. American Society for Metabolic and Bariatric Surgery www.asbs.org.
3. Mushaninga, Kuda, R.D. Nutrition and Weight Loss Surgery: An Educator's Guide. 2004.
4. Nutrition Care Manual: Gastric and Bariatric Surgery—American Dietetics Association (Accessed March 10, 2008)
5. P G Kipelman and C Grace. New Thoughts on Managing Obesity. Gut. 2004; 53(7): 1044-1053.
6. Goode, Lisa R, Brolin, Robert E., Chowdhury, Hasina A., Shapses, Sue A. Bone and Gastric Bypass Surgery: Effects of Dietary Calcium and Vitamin D. Obesity Research. 2004; 12:40-47.
7. Zittel, Tilman T., Glatzle, Jorg, Muller, Mario, Kreis, Martin, Raybould, Helen, Becker, Horst, Jehle, Ekkehard. Total Gastrectomy Severly Alters the Central Regulation of Food Intake in Rats. Ann Surg. 2002; 236(2): 166-176.
8. Brolin, Robert E. Bariatric Surgery and Long-term Control of Morbid Obesity. JAMA. 2002; 288: 2793-2796
9. Pandolfino, John E., Krishnamoorthy, Brintha, Lee, Thomas J. Gastrointestinal Complications of Obesity Surgery. MedGenMed. 2004; 6(2): 15
10. Bult, Marielle J. F., Van Dalen, Thijs, Muller, Alex F. Surgical Treatment of Obesity. European Journal of Endocrinology. 2008; 158(2): 135-145.
11. Krupa Das, Sai, Roberts, Susan B., McCrory, Megan A., Hsu, LK George, Shikora, Scott A., Kehayias, Joseph J., Dallal, Gerard E., Saltzman, Edward. Long-term Changes In Energy Expenditure and Body Composition After Massive Weight Loss Induced By Gastric Bypass Surgery. Am J Clin Nutr. 2003; 78(1): 22-30.
12. Shah, Meena, Simha, Vinaya, Garg, Abhimanyu. Long-term Impact of Bariatric Surgery on Body Weight, Comorbidities, and Nutritional Status. *Journal of Clinical Endocrinology & Metabolism*. 2006; 91(11); 4223-4231.

13. Schneider, Benjamin E., Mun, Edward C. Surgical Management of Morbid Obesity. Diabetes Care. 2005; 28: 475-480.

14. Kenler, Hallis A., Brolin, Robert E., Cody, Ronald P. Changes in Eating Behavior After Horizontal Gastroplasty and Roux-en-Y gastric bypass. *Am J Clin Nutr.* 1990; 52:87-92.

15. Fujioka, Ken. Follow-up of Nutritional and Metabolic Problems After Bariatric Surgery. Diabetes Care. 2005; 28: 481-484.

16. Brolin, R.L., Robertson, L.B., Kenler, H.A., Cody, R.P. Weight Loss and Dietary Intake After Vertical Banded Gastroplasty and Roux-en-Y Gastric Bypass. *Ann Surg.* 1994; 220(6): 782-790.

17. Olbers, Torsten, Bjorkman, Sofia, Lindroos, Ak, Maleckas, Almantas, Lonn, Lars, Sjostrom, Lars, Lonroth, Hans. Body Composition, Dietary Intake, and Energy Expenditure After Laparoscopic Roux-en-Y Gastric Bypass and Laparoscopic Verticl Banded Gastroplasty. Ann Surg. 2006; 244(5): 714-722.

18. Blackburn, George L. Solutions in Weight Control: Lessons From Gastric Surgery. *Am J Clin Nutr.* 2005; 82(1): 248S-252S.

19. Cummings, David E., Overduin, Joost, Foster-Schubert, Karen E. Gastric Bypass for Obesity: Mechanisms of Weight Loss and Diabetes Resolution. *Journal of Clinical Endocrinology & Metabolism.* 2004; 89(6): 2608-2615.

Printed in the United States
146465LV00002B/103/P

9 781436 372473